Love

The Lord your God is with you;
his power gives you victory.
The Lord will take delight in you,
and in his love he will give you new life.
He will sing and be joyful over you,
as joyful as people at a festival.

(Zephaniah 3:17-18)

To Debbie

May the Lord Bless and keep you and his face shine upon you.

Amen

SHORT STORIES TO GUIDE YOU THROUGH LIFE'S CHALLENGES AND RENEW YOUR FAITH

PRECIOUS IN HIS SIGHT

CATHERINE ANDREWS

UBUNTU COURTYARD
PUBLISHERS

Copyright © 2024 Catherine Andrews

The moral rights of the author have been asserted.

ISBN 978 -1838380823 (E-book)
ISBN 978 -1838380830 (Paperback)

First Published 2024 by Ubuntu Courtyard Publishers
A Division of Deeds of Fortune Ltd
71-75 Shelton Street,
Covent Garden,
London,
WC2H 9JQ
United Kingdom

www.ubuntucourtyard.com

All rights reserved

No part of this publication may be reproduced, stored in or introduced in a retrieval system, or transmitted, in any form or by any means (electronic, mechanical, photocopying, recording or otherwise) without the author's and publisher's prior written permission.

Unless otherwise stated, Scriptures and additional materials quoted are from the Good News Bible © 1994 published by the British and Foreign Bible Society. Good News Bible © American Bible Society 1966, 1971, 1976, 1992. Used with permission.

A CIP catalogue record for this book is available from British Library.

Editor: Fortune Mawone
Cover Design: Fortune Mawone
Typesetting and Formatting (Paperback & E-book): Vaughan Duck
www.vaughanduck.com

Chapters

1.	It's Time to Speak Of Love	1
2.	Flowers In the Valley	5
3.	He Answers	9
4.	In the Deep End	11
5.	Walking in Light	33
6.	What's Behind	39
7.	In Temporary Residence	45
8.	How Vast Is the Ocean?	55
9.	Forgiveness Is a Beautiful Thing!	59
10.	An Empty Room	63
11.	In Someone Else's Hands	69
12.	In the Valley and On the Mountain	85
13.	Are We There Yet?	87
14.	No Turning Back	101
15.	Plans to Prosper	105
16.	He Who Calms the Storm	109
17.	Time to Eat Meat	115
18.	In the Procession	119
19.	When YES means YES and NO means NO!	125

Acknowledgements

Firstly, this book is dedicated to my Lord and God, Jesus Christ, my Lord and Saviour. Who, by words I try to explain, saved me from death and took hold of me, filling me with His Holy Spirit and leading me to the point of writing this book.

I also dedicate this book to my incredible husband, two extraordinary daughters, sons-in-law, grandchildren, family and friends. Your unwavering support and love have been my anchor through life's highs and lows. I am eternally grateful for each one of you.

To Fortune Mawone, who took up the tasks of editing, publishing and all that is entailed for a book to be placed in people's hands. May God bless the work of your hands.

A great big THANK YOU to you all, my dear readers, for your support and interest in my book. Your presence in this journey means the world to me.

May the Lord bless you with His encouragement as I share uplifting words from the valleys and mountains of life.

CHAPTER ONE

It's Time To Speak Of Love

God is love. He loves us so much that He sent His only son, Jesus Christ, to give up His life so that we may have life in full.

Love is an action, not just words. The love of Christ kept Him on the cross, enduring all our pain, guilt, and shame. His love for us was so great that He suffered in a way we cannot imagine. Let us pray that the Holy Spirit will release the love of Christ within us. May God's love bring us a vision of His plans to prosper and not harm us. Remember, love never fails.

As for me, writing has become a place of refuge at times. A place of expression, sharing, and encouraging friends. Do not give up praying, do not give up reading the Word of God and do not give up asking, seeking and knocking.

Keep encouraging one another. Remember, Christ did not forget us at the cross; He remembered our weaknesses and sins. Christ Jesus remembered that without Him, we are nothing and that our Father in Heaven is glad to give us the kingdom. Our God desires to provide us with wisdom. Our Father is holy and perfect - that is what it tells me in His Word.

Let us submit to Him daily, and then we shall see His righteousness shining all over us. He gives us a gentle and humble spirit, and we shall forever be in a deep relationship with Him. Then we shall no longer be tossed about by any false doctrines, and we shall be able to stand firm in our faith, knowing full well, even in trial, our God is with us all the time.

You may be going through a test and it's uncertain when it will end. However, everything we have gone through eventually comes to an end. Every experience has a beginning and an end, and it's a great relief when the trial is over.

Dear friends, I have also gone through many trials, but my Lord brought His victory that I cannot boast of on any occasion. For it is the power of His Holy Spirit within us and all that God is, and what Jesus did at the cross that has brought victory for us. We give God the glory for granting us victory over many trials so far!

We can trust in God's love to guide us through difficult times. One of our tools is His Word, full of blessings and teachings. Through prayer, His love, and the Holy Spirit, we have been granted gifts such as grace, righteousness, tongues, healing, and knowledge about God and Jesus. With the understanding that our struggles are not against other people, we can resolve conflicts and bring about peace in any situation.

It's Time To Speak Of Love

Let us keep in mind that our struggles are spiritual. But God has given us the ability to speak positive words into our lives and situations to overcome any adversary. As the Bible states,

> *"They won the victory over him by the blood of the Lamb and by the truth which they proclaimed; and they were willing to give up their lives and die."*
>
> (Revelation 12:11)

With our mouths and belief, we can transform ourselves from within. And when God's Word penetrates our minds, souls and beings, it is like refreshing waters washing our hearts and minds.

May your Word pour forth like a never-ending river, Oh Lord. May your love wash over us and fill our hearts, even towards those who consider themselves our enemies, for you have commanded us to love them.

All through God's love for us!

Loving you, Oh Lord, as you said we should.

Great are you, Lord!

He rescues them from oppression and violence;

their lives are precious to him.

(Psalm 72:14)

CHAPTER TWO

Flowers In the Valley
A POEM

There are flowers in the valley, flowers in the mountains.

You and I are flowers that come from beauty for ashes.

Some flowers come from all devastation,
the will of God brings flowers for every occasion.

He can bring beauty from the ashes when life falls apart;
when all our hopes and dreams seem to have gone.

But God has a bigger plan and dreams for us
to dream from the ashes that the eagle rises
from His great and mighty hand.

He can take the lowest of creatures and hold them in His hand.

He can place them by His will and take them out of foreign lands.

Precious in His Sight

*He sees the broken-hearted, the poor in spirit,
the merciful, and those who mourn.*

He sees the depths of a man's heart.

*He is the Alpha and the Omega, the beginning and the end.
For the Lord has taken hold of what once was barren land.*

*He brought me water and His daily provision
from heaven above in the wilderness.
His fruits will come, and the river of life doth flow
from Christ our Lord and Saviour.*

*In Him, there is a life that we did not know.
In Him, there is a peace that this world cannot give.
In Christ, there is all that we need: forgiveness, power, love and
a clean conscience washed in the blood of Jesus Christ.*

*Like a flower in bud, He takes hold of us, and we open up to Him
as He holds us; He pours out His truth that sets us free.*

*His Word washes me like water, and it helps me grow just like
the flowers growing and bringing good fruit from His hands.*

*Oh what beauty.
Oh what love.
Oh, what a Saviour, Jesus Christ our Lord!*

Flowers in the Valley

For He has placed within this body His indestructible seed.
It is watered daily by the Word of God.

Some branches that are not bearing good fruit the Father prunes
and removes, and from there comes a new shoot that will deliver
fresh and even better fruit.

The fruit of the Holy Spirit:
Love,
peace,
patience,
kindness,
gentleness,
humility,
forgiveness and
joy in longsuffering.

Flowers bloom, yet this flesh will return to the dust one day.
It will pass away and wither like grass.
It will be seen no more, but the soul will live on.

*Yes, grass withers and flowers fade,
but the word of our God endures forever.*

(Isaiah 40:8)

CHAPTER THREE

He Answers

Includes Prayer Penned During a Difficult and Uncertain Time

Our God and King of Israel Hears and Answers!

These writings were inspired after going through a period of discouragement, wondering if God would answer prayers for our family.

And yet, the journey we are on isn't about feeling. It is about FAITH. It's about believing that what we have asked - our God has heard and will answer in His time.

And then comes someone saying that something has happened, and you realise that maybe God has heard and that what they've experienced is an answer to the prayers.

When you think you don't know what else to pray for, along comes another person with good news! They begin to speak of how their daughter's progress is going after a severe head injury; she is now doing well in recovery.

Precious in His Sight

God is so mighty we cannot fathom! His ways are far higher than ours. All we can do is TRUST that He will keep us and bring us through.

A Prayer

Do not put your servant to shame, Oh Lord and God!
Do not put your child to shame.
Oh God, lift me up in your Almighty righteous hand.
Hold me as you promised and strengthen me as you promised so that I may be able to serve others with a cheerful and grateful heart.

Strengthen this heart and establish it, Oh Lord!
Holy Spirit, strengthen me to continue to pray.

Settle my heart and help me never give up praying as your Word says - Jesus is the Son of God. I believe in the Father!
He raised His Son from the dead, and I believe in the Holy Spirit living inside this body now.

We are laying it all down to you, Jesus Christ our Lord.
We need you every moment of every day, Oh Lord Jesus.
With the help of your Holy Spirit, we ask the Holy Spirit to continue to help us and keep leading us into the truth of our Lord and God.

Thank you, Lord!

Amen.

CHAPTER FOUR

In the Deep End

PART ONE

Fear of Water

As young children, we were never acquainted with the swimming baths as they were called back in the day. Six siblings to feed and clothe meant that we didn't have the finances to visit the baths. But one particular day, my dad decided to take my eldest brother, sister and me to the baths situated in the town of Wakefield.

Dad didn't drive, so we took a bus. The journey seemed to take ages, and Wakefield then seemed miles away - another added bonus. Travelling on buses wasn't a regular occurrence for us as a family as finances did not allow such luxuries.

To this day, I remember submerging into the baths through a foot bath where we had to wash our feet before entering into what appeared to be a large pool. I was wearing a bright yellow costume which had a bubble effect on the material.

I still remember stepping out through the glass doors after walking through a foot bath; the noise of the people in the water was overwhelming. The pool looked huge, and as we came out of the changing rooms, my eyes fixed upon the deep end of the pool, which was about six or ten feet deep. It seemed too deep and dangerous for me. The thought of falling in and not being able to swim caused fear to rise up from my very being.

Well, what a shock it was when dad tried to get me to go into the shallow end of the pool. This part of the pool was about three feet tall, and my physic was always small and dainty in my younger years.

Dad tried his best to persuade me to get in the water without much luck. Eventually, I found the courage to step into the water, but not without letting out a loud scream! I couldn't take my hands off the sides; the grip was so firm there was no way my hands were going to leave the side.

Each time dad tried to persuade me to take my hands off the side, more screams of fear and anguish belted out of my mouth. The memory doesn't hold how long we were in the pool, but a remembrance of Dad leaping off the diving board into the deep end comes to mind.

As you may imagine, it was a great relief to come out of the pool, get dressed and go home. Dad never took me back again. The next time to enter the baths was during senior school, around eleven or twelve years of age.

There was no screaming this time around, but the fear of the water was still there. Fear of drowning and the very thought of my feet not touching the ground was very much present.

It took the teaching and persuasion of instructors before I could learn to swim naturally. But I was always happy to stay in the shallow end, which was the case for many more years.

We attended the baths once a week at high school which built up my confidence in the water. I even started having a go at diving which often ended up in a giant belly flop. But it was done in the deep end.

My husband of 51 years also remembers the belly flop very well. He says I was brave to have a go. As I look back, I was much more daring than I feel at times. But the fear of water always lurked in the background.

When our children were young, I did not want them to be afraid of the water. And so, I booked swimming lessons as early as possible. Our eldest daughter started lessons at eight, the youngest when she was five years old.

In six weeks, they both learnt to swim with ease. Initially, our eldest daughter was happy to stay in the shallow end, just like me when I was younger. However, as she grew older, she ventured into the deep end and swam many lengths. As for our youngest, she quickly went on to dive in and swim about ninety lengths with great confidence. All their children have no fear of water, and their aquatic skills are incredible. It is always a joy to watch them in the water.

With the right people and encouragement around us to support us in learning, we become capable and successful in that which we are being taught.

PART TWO

Confidence Building

Having confidence in anything eliminates the fear of what we are doing. Confidence can grow over time, or sometimes, it is just there.

Whilst on a family holiday, I found myself swimming with glee - from one end of the pool to the other. My aim was to deal with the fear of the deep water once and for all.

Upon reaching the deep end and the steps, I would take a deep breath and ease my body down by holding onto the steps, staying for a while and then coming back to the surface. You may wonder where this is leading to, but the story pertains to my journey of faith. It's about my experiences with my Lord and God so far.

Well, the journey of discovering the truths about God the Father, Jesus Christ and the Holy Spirit is at times like being at *the deep end.*

And we have to go deeper into the water of Word of God – the Bible. We meditate upon His Word required daily. Understanding Scripture will help us know the truth which sets us free from the many bondages we sometimes find ourselves in when, especially when we lack knowledge of who God is, Jesus Christ and the workings of the Holy Spirit. In Scripture, there is prayer and supplication, thanksgiving, sanctification, joy, praise and worship.

Diving deeper into understanding God's ways and the truth sets our minds free of the lies that the devil placed in us before we knew Christ as our Lord and Saviour.

At the start, we may feel uncomfortable and afraid. In our hearts and souls, we may feel we are in too deep and want to get out for a breather to reflect from above the water. Still, these are times when the Holy Spirit of our God and Saviour starts working within us.

Sometimes, we find ourselves in the depths of dark waters, whereby we cannot see any light, consumed with matters of the heart such as grief. But I believe our God knows how to lift us out of these waters to bring us forth into His marvellous light.

A surgeon can correct a malfunctioning heart, but no one can see the soul except for God. Only God, through His son, Jesus Christ, with the help of the Holy Spirit, can save us as sinners and give redemption to the lost and broken soul. God can restore someone's mental state to a sound and positive mindset.

PART THREE

The Lifesaver

If you fall in at the deep end of a pool or even in deep waters of the sea and ocean, you might stand a chance if you can swim. However, if you cannot swim and there is no lifeguard to save you, you will most likely drown.

We all need someone to help us in times of danger. It could be the fire service, ambulance service, lifeboat service, counselling and many other services to assist us in times of trouble.

But who can help us when our soul is in trouble?

Though we may not see it with our own eyes, the body houses the soul and spirit. It is the same soul which governs our way of thinking, and our thinking governs the soul and how it reacts to challenges in life when they come.

Now, suppose you live in an environment where critical or judgemental people discourage you from expressing yourself clearly. In that case, you are more than likely to not express your deepest emotions to them. That was the case for us as children. We were never asked how we were nor did we live in an environment where it felt safe to tell others if something horrible happened to us.

And so, we learnt to suppress emotions, and they became buried within our souls.

Personally, it took nearly 48 years before some of the incidents began to come to the surface. By then, they had festered and caused much mental anguish and uncertainty of who I was as a human being.

Now I proclaim my faith that I am who I am in Christ Jesus, and my labour has not been in vain. And yet, it is not my own personal doing but by the grace of God. Without a doubt, I believe that God stepped in and began His work to restore and rescue my soul, heal my body and strengthen my spirit.

I know it sounds too good to be true, but these hands happily type away on the keys and write about the God who created all things. He is Lord of my mind, soul and spirit and governor of my body. He has become my lifeguard, rescuer, trainer, psychologist and counsellor. He is the same God who restored someone like me from a dead place. He can do the same for you and anyone else.

To Him only is the glory for the power of His works within us. Some people in life need God to rescue them. They need to know about Jesus Christ, His Son, what happened, and why at the cross at the Cavalry. Some people need a transformation of mind, spirit, soul and body.

And ALL things are possible with God!

I hope you know that we can receive healing, understanding, and knowledge through Jesus Christ and His work at the cross. But most of all, may we receive everlasting love into our hearts and peace that surpasses all understanding.

Through the continuing study of the Bible - God's Word, we can learn how to live and treat others in a better way and how to react toward those who hate us.

Jesus Christ is the anchor of our souls and lifesaver.

Hallelujah!

PART FOUR

Starting in the Shallow End

As the Holy Spirit of God works in us, we are taken deeper and deeper as God draws closer to us. We begin to develop a deep and intimate relationship with God through Jesus Christ and the Holy Spirit. Diving into deep waters with God means letting go of what once was familiar as He becomes more relevant. And the more we see and experience who He is, the more we praise Him from the heart.

> *"Praise the Lord!*
> *Praise the Lord from heaven,*
> *you that live in the heights above.*
> *Praise him, all his angels,*
> *all his heavenly armies.*
>
> *"Praise him, sun and moon;*
> *praise him, shining stars.*
> *Praise him, highest heavens,*
> *and the waters above the sky.*

In the Deep End

"Let them all praise the name of the Lord!
He commanded, and they were created;
by his command they were fixed in their places forever,
and they cannot disobey.

"Praise the Lord from the earth,
sea monsters and all ocean depths;
lightning and hail, snow and clouds,
strong winds that obey his command.

"Praise him, hills and mountains,
fruit trees and forests;
all animals, tame and wild,
reptiles and birds.

"Praise him, kings and all peoples,
princes and all other rulers;
young women and young men,
old people and children too.

"Let them all praise the name of the Lord!
His name is greater than all others;
his glory is above earth and heaven.
He made his nation strong,
so that all his people praise him—
the people of Israel, so dear to him.

"Praise the Lord!" (Psalm 148:1-14)

As I spend time reading the Bible, it sometimes feels as if I'm dipping my toes and stepping in towards the deep end.

With encouragement and persuasion from the prompting of the Holy Spirit through His Word of Truth – it feels like water at times washing my spirit, soul and body.

As I open up my heart and mind, it feels as if I'm diving in at the deep end, looking around under the water for treasure beneath the depths of God's Word. It paved the way for God to manifest. As a child of God, being obedient allows Him to reside within and closer to us as we glorify His name.

Hallelujah!

To make something clean or pure can take time. For those who believe in Christ and God the Father who sent Him comes the washing and sanctifying through the blood of Jesus Christ. It has been made possible for us to go to God and Father and be redeemed through the blood of Jesus Christ.

The Word and Truth of God's Word are described as living waters. They are alive and can bring life back into the body with the help of the Holy Spirit.

Jesus has made way for us to be reconciled back to God and learn to have an intimate relationship with Him. We are relying upon God for our lives and all that the new life in Christ entails.

For Jesus Christ was victorious at the cross, and He did it all for us that we might be saved by God's grace for all eternity to live with Him once our fleshly body is no more. Consider the following verse:

In the Deep End

> *"Since this is true, how much more is accomplished by the blood of Christ! Through the eternal Spirit he offered himself as a perfect sacrifice to God. His blood will purify our consciences from useless rituals, so that we may serve the living God."*
>
> (Hebrews 9:14)

Sin is heavy and pulls us down. Sin brings confusion and removes our identity of who God planned us to be before sin entered the world through Adam and Eve. Let us look at another Bible verse to help us understand why we need sanctification:

> *"Elisha sent a servant out to tell him to go and wash himself seven times in the Jordan River, and he would be completely cured of his disease."*
>
> (2 Kings 5:10)

This passage of Scripture regards Naaman, who had leprosy. Naaman went to the house of Elisha for healing. He was the captain of the host of the king of Syria and described as a great man with his master and honourable because the Lord had given deliverance unto Syria by him.

As Naaman approached the door of Elisha's home, Elisha sent a messenger to Naaman with a message to go and wash himself in the Jordan River seven times so that he would be healed. The number seven is considered significant in the Bible in relation to God's works.

But Naaman expects Elisha to come to him and call upon

the name of the Lord and strike His hand and heal Naaman of leprosy. His servants persuade him to do as Elisha had said. Indeed, Naaman goes to the river and dips himself seven times. He is healed of leprosy.

Throughout history, people were cleansed with water and forgiven of sins by sacrificing blood being shed in the Bible. The Old Testament was the sacrifice of a lamb or goat. The New Testament by which we now live in came about through the sacrifice of Christ's blood. We no longer need to kill a lamb or goat to forgive our sins.

In the Old Testament, people were cleansed with water and forgiven of sins through sacrificing the blood of a lamb. Goats became scapegoats to pave the way for the atonement of sins. But the New Testament by which we now live in came about through the sacrifice of Christ's blood. Through Jesus Christ, our sins are forgiven when we repent and accept Him as Lord and Saviour.

That is my encouragement as a believer in Christ Jesus. I believe God does hear our prayers and requests. It is up to Him as to when and how He will answer them.

David, the Psalmist who became the king of Israel, wrote:

> *"Remove my sin, and I will be clean; wash me, and I will be whiter than snow."* (Psalm 51:7)

Other Biblical translations mention hyssop, which was a plant used for purification sprinkling, a cleansing agent. It was used to purge, cleanse or purify. We too can find purification as we delve deeper into the Word of God and nurture an intimate relationship with Him.

But as the years have gone by, the Word has taken me deeper into the hurts and pains. God's Word, with the help of His Holy Spirit has enabled me to hand over many regrets, pain and wounds in my soul, learning to trust in Jesus Christ as my Lord and Saviour. He gave His life for me because He loved me.

And He loves you too, the reader of these writings. I've trusted the Lord with them, and He has brought healing and relieved me of disappointment, guilt and shame, regret and anger, frustration and bitterness.

Oh, I thank God every day for the newness of life through His Son Jesus Christ who gave His life for the world because He loved us!

I started my faith journey from the shallow end, but was eventually thrown in at the deep end. I had to learn how to rise above every challenge in life so far:

To swim to the top of the pool to catch our breath. On this journey with Christ Jesus, there are times when I sit and do nothing except reflect upon what God has done – meditating upon His Word.

This process is like floating on top of the waters, relaxing and allowing the waters to hold you up, with minimal effort from the physical body.

Eventually, calmness returns inside and God's peace which transcends all understanding arises. Transcend means above ALL knowledge. We can find rest in that place from all the things of this world. And over time, I have been healed of anger, bitterness and many other life's frustrations.

PART FIVE

The Strengthening of the Swim

Having related this walk with Jesus Christ with water and a swimming pool or the ocean, I pray it will be of encouragement to someone as they deal with many life's challenges.

May I remind you of the first time entering the baths with Dad? Fear, screaming and being frightened were the order of the day. I just couldn't wait to get out of the water.

Slowly, I have enjoyed swimming in a pool and have become more adapted to jumping in. I still hold my nose though – that feeling when water goes inside the nostrils is not something that feels comfortable for me. But with the persuasion of a professional instructor, swimming slowly became something I could do with confidence.

A few years ago, consideration was made as to whether diving lessons would be a good idea to take me to another level of overcoming water.

It is an ongoing progression to overcome the fear of the

breaststroke or learning to dive in at the deep end of the pool. I have sought the help of instructors to help me overcome entering deep waters.

Now, in this walk with God and learning about why Jesus Christ was crucified, resurrected, ascended to heaven and will once more come again under the authority of God the Father, there has been a need and still is the need for an instructor. They teach and help me become a stronger swimmer against life's many tides.

If you are a river swimmer for some reason, you will know about tidal currents under the waters. Have you ever had to swim against the tidal current? What about the salmon who once a year has to swim against the tidal current to spawn its eggs for future salmon?

Now, although physically, I've never swam against any tidal current, my first thought is that you must be a powerful swimmer to do so. Maybe there is a daily routine of building up strength in the arms and legs that you need to do and perfect. Perhaps there is a different technique for swimming against the tide.

I've observed how those who swim to great lengths and noticed something interesting. Their shoulders appear wider than those of us who do not swim long distances. Some cross the English Channel, and some float in races in the Olympic games.

Walking by faith in Christ Jesus is like swimming against the tide as the body's flesh is currently being trained to walk another way, opposite to how the world sees things at times.

For example, if someone has wronged you, wouldn't you want to treat them the same way? Would you forgive them and tell them so, or would you seek revenge by not talking to them anymore or contemplating doing the same thing they did to you?

The world is full of opinions, with everyone willing to weigh in with their ideas. Many people go to any lengths to give their opinion. But what if the view brings strife and does not resolve peace?

What if the opinion causes someone to fall into sin? Sin is quite severe and not something to be taken lightly. Sin is the most profound thing in the entire world. It causes people to hate one another, fight with one another, causes families to break up and bring heartache and despair. It causes marriages to break up. Children run away from home and live on the streets. These are just a few of the fruits that come from sin.

And God hates liars. I believe there is no such thing as a white lie. A lie is a lie.

When I learnt through Scripture that God hates liars, it woke me up from spiritual sleep and led me to confess my sin. I learnt that my fear was of men and what they would do to me if I told the truth. Through the FEAR OF MAN, not God, I had told many lies as a child to adulthood. And many people find themselves in these situations today. But FEAR OF THE LORD is the beginning of wisdom.

I am thankful that my Father Has rescued me from the dominion of darkness, from Satan's kingdom and bringing me into the realm of His beloved Son where through His blood - there is redemption and forgiveness of all my sins.

The Lord is my helper. What can I do to myself? If God is for me, then who can be against me?

May we consider these words daily that so that it will help to treat one another as God would love us to do - with love, gentleness, kindness, and forgiveness.

And the Lord will be our daily portion, filling our mouths with good things and loading us daily with His benefits of peace, love and power to overcome temptations and trials through Jesus Christ.

In the name of Jesus, I pray to the Father that this would be for you, dear reader.

When we are in the dark, we cannot see what is in the room with us. When God brings you into His light, the light shines inside and reveals what has been hidden in your heart. No one can live for long in that place, for darkness destroys a person's soul and personality. It may even take someone's life through illness. It took me decades of suffering through bitterness and resentment until I saw the light. The darkness would have taken my life had it not been for the Lord. He took hold of me with His invisible hand and led me out of the darkest of places into His light.

These writings are inspired by my personal experiences which led to my fear of the Lord. It gave me wisdom to understand that I'm nothing but dust without Him.

With Him and through Jesus Christ and the power of the Holy Spirit, God now gives me assignments to do. With His strength, wisdom and knowledge, He enables me to do them.

It never occurred to my mind that one day, I would become a writer of such wonderful things about God. It was never part of my plan. However, it was God's plan so I could be an encourager to others. I believe that at this time in life, my role is to share truths about my God. In His greatness, He has done many wonders for me! I pray that in this life, you too can taste and see that the Lord is indeed good and proclaim it with your mouths. The more we share the GOOD NEWS, the more we encourage others to walk from the shallow end, to the deep end; a place where our thirsts are quenched with living waters which do not dry up.

PART SIX

Staying Afloat

How then do we stay afloat on the journey of discovery of Christ Jesus? How do I continue to carry out the assignments that God has ordained for me to do before leaving this life for good?

The assignments are to tell others of the true and living God!

In the Deep End

That Jesus loves them and that He gave His life and shed His blood for us so that we may come to know Him as our Lord and Saviour; be in an intimate relationship with God and be at peace with God through Jesus Christ.

To stay afloat and focused upon God and by faith in Jesus Christ daily, there is a need to continue in prayer, humbling myself before the Lord, submitting to God for His will to be done and then thanking Him. It means regular praise and worship, as well as bringing supplications and requests before God for other people.

My prayer is for souls to be saved by God's grace and kept for the kingdom of heaven.

The reading of the Bible daily encourages me to keep going, for the Lord Jesus will come again when the Father says so, with the angels and a trumpet sound to bring His people home into heaven with Him for all eternity. I believe we will see His face one day, with a light so bright we will be singing *"Holy, Holy, Holy is the Lord God Almighty!"* There is no one like God, no one.

I believe in staying afloat, becoming calm within, strengthened by His Holy Spirit. He teaches truth and speaks the truth. The Holy Spirit cannot lie as He is the Spirit of God. The Holy Spirit guides the truth about Jesus Christ and why he died on the cross for us because he loved us. The Holy Spirit reveals Christ as our spiritual husband to bring us eternal life once this fleshly body passes away.

By the power of God's works within us, He will one complete His works for His glory.

Oh, my heart sings and hopes that God will reveal these truths to my husband, children, sons-in-law, grandchildren, brothers, sisters, brothers-in-law, sisters-in-law, nephews and nieces, including all relatives and friends who I've ever known or will know. For there is only ONE God, seated in heaven on His throne with His Son, our Lord Jesus Christ - the ruler of heaven and earth. And the kingdom of heaven shall be the only kingdom that will remain forever and ever.

Our journeys of faith sometimes mean we are thrown in at the deep end or begin in the shallow end; building confidence to go deeper into God's truth - like living water that washes our souls, minds, hearts, and spirit clean. There is no greater God than the God and Father of our Lord Jesus Christ: One Lord, one faith, one baptism and one Holy Spirit of God. And so, we proclaim that Jesus Christ is Lord.

Hallelujah!

I pray that these writings to encourage others to start somewhere, even if it means a shallow end. Over time, you will gain more confidence and understanding of His Word to help you swim to the top, strengthen the swim of faith in Christ Jesus, even if you may be questioning and doubting if what is written is true. Ask for guidance and understanding.

My hope is for souls to be saved all eternity with Christ. What a beautiful name is the Lord Jesus Christ.

CONCLUSION

Whether we dive in at the deep end and learn to swim to the top, or whether we begin in the shallow end - dipping in our feet until we are ready to go deeper, be reassured that God is with us every step of the way. Remember that even when it feels as if you're staying afloat or swimming against the tide, you're not alone.

He has promised in Scripture that God's Word cannot fail. He has never failed and God's love for us will not fail us, and His faithfulness will not fail us. Thank God we have a God who knows ALL things. He knows every part of our being. He knows where He is going to take us.

To God, alone who is wise, be the glory through Jesus Christ for ever!

Amen.

The Lord is my light and my salvation;

I will fear no one.

The Lord protects me from all danger;

I will never be afraid.

When evil people attack me and try to kill me,

they stumble and fall.

(Psalm 27:1-2)

CHAPTER FIVE

Walking in Light

There is a light brighter than the sun. It's brighter than the moon and, as yet, cannot be seen by the naked eye but is experienced through our spiritual sight. For Jesus Christ is the light of the world. He came to live and die here on earth for us. He lived as a man - experiencing the world, its cruelty and wickedness. Jesus suffered profusely.

God the Father placed upon Jesus's shoulders all the sins of the world, and He bled and died for us. His blood is pure, and His life was of no wrong. And yet, He chose to be obedient unto death to His Father to the end. And now we can find peace and solace for our souls in Jesus Christ. We can have a new life.

My encouragement today is to accept Him and receive Jesus into your hearts right now.

To truly understand Jesus Christ, we need the guidance of His Holy Spirit. Without it, we may find ourselves trapped in a cycle of sin that leads us deeper and deeper into darkness. But God is light, and His presence reveals our sins. Though this can be a painful process, it leads to repentance and a newfound awareness of the seriousness of our actions. As we turn away from our old ways, we may feel a sense of self-loathing. But ultimately, this transformation leads us closer to the truth of who Jesus Christ is.

When God takes control of your life, a transformation occurs. Those activities and behaviors that once brought you joy, such as excessive drinking and engaging in lustful and deceitful conduct begin to lose their appeal. You start to feel a sense of depletion and guilt, but this is all part of God's plan. By shedding these harmful habits, you open up to a new, more fulfilling life.

For God causes us to repent and turn to Him. We begin to know the truth, the seriousness of sin, and its effects on our lives. Being deceived by the devil only leads us into sin. We may not know it is happening until the light comes and wakes us up from a spiritual sleep, and Oh boy, are you woken up!

From here on, things begin to change, and there might be deep suffering as God begins to change us. A deep mourning and sadness may at first appear. Do not be afraid, for God is working in you, dear. His Holy Spirit searches us day and night, and we begin to hate sin so much we begin to cry out:

"Help me, Lord! Rid me of this sin, wash me and cleanse me with your blood that is pure and clean."

God may have to take you to deeper places in yourself, for the root of bitterness may have established itself in your soul. Anger and rage may sometimes come forth. Still, do not be discouraged, for God is working everything out. What you'd become inside may appear on the outside, and things might get worse as the festering wounds begin to be cleansed of their puss.

Sometimes, you may think I can't stand this anymore, and yet, the Holy Spirit of God will reveal God's truth to you. We begin to realise that God is purging our conscience clean through the blood of Jesus. He is washing us clean - our souls, minds and hearts.

And all God's ways are not ours; He has a way like no other. We come to a point where we don't want to sin anymore, yet the fleshly body fights with the spirit.

But God has a way of helping us overcome through Jesus Christ, the light of the world. Accept Him and ask Him to live in your heart. Pray that the Lord seat himself between your sin and make you all you have been called to be – to be of good service to our God who saves. And by His grace we are saved! As the song clearly says, "Amazing grace, how sweet the sound that saved a wretch like me...'

We hear of cancer and many other diseases, but the most significant is a silent disease. It is a disease of the heart in the sinful man. Sin is a disease that only God can remove through the blood of Jesus Christ; He is able to wash us clean. Sin hides in the darkest depths of our hearts, but when the light of Christ comes in, sin can no longer hide.

We begin to hate sin the same way God does. We hate the things God hates, all kinds of evil - we begin to hate. Still, the devil comes to tempt us to try and prevent us from living for Christ. But be encouraged because if God is in you by His Holy Spirit, He will always help you overcome all evil. One day, you will realise you are in God's light, free from fear and living for Jesus Christ, longing for the day you will see Him face to face.

At present, it feels as though we are peering into a mirror, envisioning our future selves just as we will be when Jesus Christ comes to bring us to our heavenly home.

As believers, we recognise that our true home is no longer in this world. Instead, we find our belonging in God, our loving Father, faithful friend, and righteous King. Through fellowship with Him and the guidance of the Holy Spirit, we are empowered to overcome sin and receive the cleansing power of Christ's blood. His Word shines upon our path and fills us with courage, even in the darkest of times. We take comfort in knowing that the Lord God Almighty is always by our side, and we need not fear as we journey through this life.

The self has to die in order for the new creation to come. He who is faithful will do it for you.

He will cause you to hunger for God's truth, and He will cause you to delight in His glorious light. May the glory of the Lord shine upon you this day!

May we always remain in the embrace of God's radiant light

and be liberated by His grace. Let us strive to follow in His footsteps and serve our fellow beings just as He has served us. Jesus did not come to this world seeking to be served. His mission was to selflessly help others to fulfil His Father's will. May it be done on earth as it is in heaven.

The life of Jesus never ceases to amaze me. In the short span of time He spent on earth, Jesus demonstrated God's love to the world. He cared for others, even washing their feet. He had compassion for the forsaken, hopeless and downtrodden. He healed the sick and freed the tormented. He cared for the widows and fed the poor and orphans. Remarkably, even when faced with persecution and physical abuse from the people he came to save, He didn't retaliate. He instead forgave them, saying, "Father forgive them, for they do not know what they do."

As we strive to walk in the light, may we be illuminated, guided, and guarded by His divine light. Without it, we will not find the way.

In Jesus's Name.

Amen.

✟

―――――――――――――――――――――――

Let us give thanks to the God and Father
of our Lord Jesus Christ!
For in our union with Christ he has blessed us by giving us
every spiritual blessing in the heavenly world.

(Ephesians 1:3)

CHAPTER SIX

What's Behind

Through the Holy Spirit of my Lord and God, it is as if the Lord helps me to understand His works within us. He has plans for us to prosper, but in those plans, there may be a time when something within us needs to be stripped down for the new to come and be placed securely to last forever into eternity. The inspiration behind this story came as we prepared to renovate our old kitchen.

May I say in the fifty years of marriage, we have never been through this process. Had the process been ten years earlier, I would not have coped with the trauma of it all. The process has been pleasant and not at all traumatic. Surely this must be the Lord's doing.

The Bible says He chose me before the foundations of the world. Therefore, He knew the time that my frail body would come forth out of my mother's womb. He knew which family to put me in and knew the day he would stretch out His right and victorious hand to save me from a sinful existence.

The Lord has always had a plan, and yet, my eyes could not see that plan nor did my mind know of any plans that God had for me to save me as a young mother of two children. Much work has been done where no one has seen: internal preparation and much work to be done to heal and restore my soul to my King. My soul belongs to Him - King of Glory!

It belongs to no one else, but my Lord and King Jesus Christ came to save my soul to live on with Him forever.

The plans for the kitchen have taken over a year. There's been much deciding about the colour scheme, what was needed to fit in, where to go and who to ask for many jobs to be done before the new kitchen materialised. There have been unseen works that we could only see once the old kitchen was entirely removed.

We had discussions with the Water Board, plumber, electrician and plasterer before the fitter could start his job, followed by the floor fitter and decorator. We've taken many trips to the tip; getting rid of the old as we prepared for the new. A skip for this and that, a skip for each piece of the rubbish disposed of in the right place.

I couldn't help but remember when my Lord first revealed His Glory through crucifixion. Our sins were as red as scarlet, but His blood washed away all our sins. There was so much rubbish to get rid of; the work on the cross – just like renovation - was as painful as something was truly being ripped out. Of course, it was because the old had to be crucified.

What's Behind

God already knows the final work within us because of His love. He knows what goes on behind the scenes. Nothing can separate me from His love.

As the kitchen began its transformation stages, we saw with our eyes what was going on behind the scenes before the finished products were all in - boxes yet to be revealed as the builder opened them. Doesn't this bring a reflection that the Lord is with us? His Holy Spirit - the light within us shining into the areas within our hearts and souls. The places that need to be restored and renewed.

Christ our Master, the precious stone, the foundation of the faith our God gave us, the MASTER BUILDER giving out instructions on how to heal and restore our souls. Much work goes on behind the scenes for the salvation of our souls. We ask, and then, we have to wait for the prayer to be manifested here on earth. Our times are in God's hands.

He is the owner of the universe. He has set the tides to pass over their boundaries. He sends a gale and a storm, yet in it all, He also calms the storm and stops the sea from covering the earth as was in the days of Noah.

There are rumours of wars, and raging forces are in battle, And yet, the Lord said, DO NOT be afraid of all these things. Do not be scared of earthquakes and famine. They are all the birth pains for the new heaven and earth that will one day come. A city of light! The new Jerusalem is where all God's people will live with Him.

As the work in the kitchen continued, demolition work first got rid of the old that had to be thrown away. It led to the preparation for the new kitchen, a process whereby each skilled worker did the job they had been trained for. The plumber, electrician, plasterer, fitter, builder and decorator all played different roles as if to restore the temple of Christ. Outsiders didn't see all this work being carried out, except for the owners, who could only marvel at the jobs behind the scenes. Others would only admire the finished work later on, when the work had been finished.

To finally bring forth a total transformation of what was once a rotting kitchen, damp and without much attraction brought us so much joy. And yet, despite its not so – attractive state, the very old kitchen and stove served the owners, family and others well with many years of home-cooked meals!

May this new season of change still bring food for those who need it, wherever it's coming from. A meal cooked with love and a place to refresh beats a designer kitchen every time. May the new oven and hob serve God for His Glory to bring people together to receive Christ our Lord and Saviour.

Dials have changed, and the power has switched from gas to electric. There will be a time of learning. It will take time to adapt to the new as the mind gets used to new ways of cooking. It's the same with God, who has brought us out of darkness into His light.

There is a time for demolition and tear down and then to build from the Word of our Lord and God. There are times of instruction and teaching, a time to introduce new things and learning how the new things work. There is also a time to apply the new teachings once we know how to. We need the master planner to show us how. We need to trust in the builder that is the Lord; there may be times when walls are pulled down - walls within our hearts. The kind of walls that separate us from the love of God and being able to experience and share God's perfect love with His people. There is nothing our God does not know and nothing He can't do. He has promised never to leave us; His grace is sufficient. His love will never fail us.

It is painful when the old part of us is being torn down and crucified, but God said he would be with us in times of trouble, and He delivers us from all our troubles.

One truth reminding me to keep my eyes on Jesus - with hope, during those painful moments is that God says DO NOT be angry, for it leads to evil. Do not get mad, dear brother and sister, if God has not answered your prayer. For it is written: God does not slack in answering prayers. There may be other people that God has to work with before your prayer comes forth. It's painful being crucified, but the most painful of deaths was when our Lord Jesus Christ was nailed on the cross so that we might be saved.

Our trials come in different forms – which aren't physical the way Jesus died on the cross. But still, I believe that sometimes, the pain we feel is the old part of the old - self being crucified with Christ. It is written:

Precious in His Sight

To be made alive in Christ and being born again is to be an image of our Christ, a reflection and imitator of God. To gain this status, we have to be crucified inside ourselves, corrected by the builder who knows what He is doing. After that, a cleaner and better – functioning YOU is revealed.

May God your Glorious Father of our Lord Jesus Christ, in His name and for His Glory give us mercy, grace, wisdom and understanding as He prunes our hearts today.

Glory to the MASTER BUILDER of our faith who heals us from all our pain, sickness and disease!

Glory to the Lord who restores our souls and brings them to a place of rejoicing!

To God be the Glory and to Jesus Christ, His Son!

To God be the Glory forever and ever!

Amen.

CHAPTER SEVEN

In Temporary Residence

In a temporary residence, that is where we are - our body being a temporary covering of who we really are. For the Spirit of God is inside us. It is written that Christ is in us, and we are in Christ.

Therefore our true home is with Him, the one who gave His life so that we might come to know our Lord and God. To be in relationship with Him, moment by moment, day after day, being led in procession by the Lord Jesus Chris. He is leading us home out of this world that will be no more.

Oh, there have been days when the longing has been to be with my Saviour - in His arms to be!

The flesh will fight against the Holy Spirit sometimes, and a call (prayer) to the one who knows the person in residence saves the day.

Lord and King, Saviour and God!

He always comes forth and lifts me. His instructions as we live in this temporary place are to love one another deeply, forgive, help and pray for one another.

My body has become a temple of the Holy Spirit and my God. I search my heart and mind, trying to find who God says I am, as His child. God is my Father and Jesus Christ my Lord and Saviour, the Holy Spirit teaching the truth about my Lord.
Like a child, I keep coming to the Father, calling upon my Saviour!
Jesus Christ is the name of my best friend.

When no one else has been there in the night, my Saviour has been there for me.
The Holy Spirit of my Father and God fills my mouth and calls out to my Lord and God as this body lays still in the early hours of the dawn - listening to the Word of my Lord. He feeds me bread from heaven; His Word is pure and brings peace to my soul.

A longing of my soul at times to be at rest - eyes closed and meditating upon the Word of my Lord and God.

"Do not be discouraged," a voice in the distance is heard.
"I hold you with my right and victorious hand. Do not fear."

Oh, help me through this valley!
The Lord's right-hand holds and leads me.
His eyes can see my future better than I.

In Temporary Residence

God has good things and removes the mountains for me.

The owner of this body is now my God.
He purchased every cell, tissue, mind, body, soul and spirit with the precious blood of Jesus Christ, His Son.

The old resident sometimes tries to break in and take over, but the Spirit of the Lord is much more robust in me. He speaks truth to the lies that try to take control, and they then have to go eventually. Peace once more, resting in the Lord, meditating upon His Word.

Much goes off in the place of residence; there have been many changes over the last 69 years. There was a time when it appeared the demolition team had moved in, every room stripped bare and the wind blowing in.
Roof taken off, windows blown out - not much left after the demolition team moved out.

But along came a builder, His name I did not know.
He offered to help build the house once more!
He took hold of my hand and said, "Tell yourself you will get well."

At first, I didn't trust the builder of this new house; it all seemed strange.
And yet, He seemed so kind, never losing His temper or forcing me to do anything I wasn't ready to do.

There came a time when He said you need a manual so you can study the builder who has come to give you life, unlike the destroyer who tried to take your life - being led into all kinds of temptations and pits.

"He was leading you to your final destruction by digging holes so that you will fall into them.

He is so cunning and evil that he doesn't care to reveal what kind of destroyer he is.

His cunningness makes people think they are doing well, pride taking the centre stand."

"Look at me, how well I've done!"
Mouth like a sewer pit gossiping about others.
Falling deeper into the pit, it became so dark that life was almost snuffed out.
The destroyer destroyed every room of the house, but my Lord and God had a better plan to renovate, build, and heal the broken parts.

I give thanks for His name - Jesus Christ, my Lord and Saviour!
He is called many names.
He said I AM the Alpha and Omega; the author and finisher of this new life.
You need to rest and let the builder build.
Listen to the instructions as we walk together with the truth and words of my book.

A hunger came to read the manual, a desire to know more about the builder holding me.
He has a Father who is holy and true.

In Temporary Residence

He has sent another helper - the Holy Spirit of God.

The building was so destroyed it has taken many years to trust and allow the builder to take control and build.
At first, I tried to hide in the smallest of corners - too afraid to trust in this man called Jesus; He had come to save.
Shaking, trembling, fear of everything.
How would I ever live life again?
Husband by my side, but God was in control.
Children were only young; they needed a mother.
Each day without knowing, the Lord became my strength.
And yet, I didn't even know it.
The darkest valley no - one could ever imagine, yet a glimpse of light showed me the way.

So while I lay down, He would meet me there, caressing me with sweet words, telling me not to fear.
Much confusion, that's all I had.
How could this builder finish what He began to do?

After a while, He said, "You need to be baptised, washed, justified and sanctified to move into a better place to live. I will send you another helper, and He will teach you about me."

OK! Where will that be?
In a pool of water - submerged for a moment.
To wash away the old thoughts and help you develop new ones.

It still took a while for me to learn to trust who this person was; so kind, gentle, patient and ready to help whenever I called.

Even in the stillness of the night, He was there.

He has been with me every step of the way and will be faithful until the end.

Like a night nurse always there to hold my hand and calm me down as the enemies tried to pull me down.

Nightmares and sweats many have been, not fully knowing what has been.

But I do know the new builder who came to help that day.

He has never once left nor forsaken me.

He has taken away all my fears.

And when my heart feels downcast, He always lifts me.

Longing for the joy that He describes in His manual, a deep love has developed between my builder and me.

Each night I lie down and trust in my builder to help me dwell in safety until the morning comes.

Many nights are spent just with my builder and me, talking things through and giving Him the dream that He may take it into captivity.

Lay there thinking about the words that He has taught me, waiting for the morning to go forth with my builder and tell others, pointing them to Jesus Christ, Lord and Saviour of this world.

Jesus Christ is the name of my builder.

In Temporary Residence

He is Lord, and God is His Father of all.
God is now my Father, for the manual says He is.
He saved me from destruction and a fiery pit.

The temporary residence is more authentic now than when the builder began.
There are still parts of the building that seem in need of repair and refurbishment.
But I'm not letting go of my builder, and He isn't letting go of me.
He said you are precious to me.
This work that I've begun I will complete.
Remain in the manual, and the words will remain in you so that you know that I am for you and not against you.
I've come to give a better life than the destroyer ever did.
He had no intention of ever freeing you from the pit.

But I am the Great I AM!
Nothing is impossible for me.
I AM the master builder, and no one can overpower me.
No weapon, demon, angel, trial or temptation can overcome me.
Therefore you are now an overcomer.
Through me, I have overcome for you in the secret place.

Look back for me and see what I have done.
I was always with you, even in your mother's womb.
I was there to see that you were born again, not out of your mother's womb but through Christ my Son, and sealed you

with the Holy Spirit for such a time as this.
Even in old age, your builder will be with you.
It has cost me nothing for this new life through Christ, for Christ Jesus, my Lord and Saviour has paid the bill.

"It is wise to let go," He said one day.
So many times have I meditated on those words, once knowing that I was forgiven and LOVE came in like a flood. But it appeared I gave that to the pigs, not understanding the significance of what the builder had just done.

Like Moses, maybe that was a poignant moment, perhaps a test I didn't know.
But the builder is still with me and helps me each day, moulding and shaping each room on the way.

Some rooms still need renovating as there appears at times something in need of a clean and shine.
Still, the builder is always there.
Do you know Him?
Can I give you His name?
He is ready to help you with your repairs!

Jesus is His name, Christ Jesus our Lord and Saviour.
There is no number to call - you call Him by His name.
He says He is always awake to take our call; it costs no money.
Just our time to sit and listen to what He has to say in His time.
He may or may not answer all our questions one day.

In Temporary Residence

But My trust in Him grows stronger each day.
Without Him, there will be no eternal heavenly place, my final resting place in heaven with Him.
The day will come when He will take away my soul's and spirit's last breath in the hope of eternal life with my God.

I shall not struggle as I see His light.
For I believe God will give me the strength for this body till I die.
The body is only a temporary place of covering.
A day will come; that is my hope.
A new body is given, becoming like Jesus Christ.
For now, it is like looking in a glass and seeing an image of my Lord Jesus Christ, with the help of His Holy Spirit.
Making me an image of Jesus Christ in this temporary place of living.

What a glorious day when we shall see His face.
I hope He will say well done, good and faithful servant!

> *"To him who is able to keep you from falling, and to bring you faultless and joyful before his glorious presence — to the only God our Saviour, through Jesus Christ our Lord, be glory, majesty, might, and authority, from all ages past, and now, and or ever and ever! Amen."* (Jude 1:24-5)

The grace of our Lord Jesus Christ be with you all.

Amen.

Aren't five sparrows sold for two pennies?
Yet not one sparrow is forgotten by God.
Even the hairs of your head have all been counted.
So do not be afraid; you are worth much more
than many sparrows!

(Luke 12:6-7)

CHAPTER EIGHT

How Vast Is the Ocean?
A Moment of Reflection Whilst on Holiday

How vast is the ocean? How wide is the sea? How many grains of sand can we see?

No one knows except for God himself. He knows everything to the very depths of the sea. Have we seen the depths? Did we swim to the bottom? Can we count the grains of sand? No is the answer. And yet, our Lord and God know—He who created everything in the sea, the maker of heaven and earth.

He created you and me.

Our Creator, God, not only provides for all creatures in the sea but also holds us with His victorious hand and guides us toward eternal life. He encourages us to ask, seek and knock and we shall receive, find, and the door will be open for us.

As we looked down from the seat above, the sea became calm like a mill pond. People were splashing in the ocean, and dogs were running around freely. I could hear the birds chirping and seagulls squeaking. In the distance, I could also hear traffic and nearby trees rustling in the sunshine. Ahead of us was a hotel where the staff worked hard to ensure our stay was enjoyable.

We took in the fresh and clean air, relaxed and listened to the songs of someone singing. People of different shapes and sizes passed by; toddlers, babies, older and frail ones. Some needing help with their wheelchairs, and at times, some needing support and assistance with a gentle hand.

Some seemed more vulnerable than others and in need of a hug or someone to steady and guide them. This reminds me that as different as we are, and even though we all have gone through different experiences in life, we all need others to help us. We need assistance with many things, and yet, sometimes, we think we need no one and can easily do everything on our own.

How stubborn, at times, human nature can be! However, it's important to remember that God requires us to submit to Him. By so doing, we allow Him to demonstrate His strength in our weakness.

The moment I think I don't need anyone, weakness comes. I am reminded that in this body of flesh, I need God to help me and others to come along to help fulfil God's work here on earth.

Thank God for Christ Jesus, for in Him and through Him and the Holy Spirit of our God, we are able to do all things through Jesus Christ, our Lord and Saviour.

How vast is our God?

How Vast Is the Ocean?

We can never know until eternity, and then maybe we will know!

Help us, dear Lord, not to limit you with our minds. Please help us serve you. Open our minds to your unlimited plans to prosper and not harm us. We ask these things in Jesus's name. Help us fulfil what you would want us to do and where you require us to be each day. We acknowledge our dependence on your love and support; without it, we are nothing but meaningless sound. Thank you for your unwavering presence in our lives.

Oh, Son of God, we glorify you and exalt your name. You are worthy of all worship and praise, my Lord and God.

May your name be honoured and revered always.

Amen.

―――――――――――――――― ✝ ――――――――――――――――

*If you forgive others the wrongs they have done to you,
your Father in heaven will also forgive you.*

(Matthew 6:14)

CHAPTER NINE

Forgiveness Is a Beautiful Thing!

Forgiveness is a beautiful thing.

It is more precious than any jewel.

Forgiveness is one of the most extraordinary things, for it comes from pure love.

Forgiveness is a gift, so let it be opened up and not placed in the drawer or a cupboard. The more we use it, the more it grows, and it becomes easier as we apply it to our hearts. Let us utilise that gift of forgiveness for others. As Jesus was crucified, He gave the world another gift: "Forgive them, Father, for they do not know what they do."

Has not God the Father forgiven us through Jesus Christ, His blood and sacrifice?

And yet Jesus said if we don't forgive others, God will not forgive us.

Oh, the gift of forgiveness is pure! It is clean and brings forth light and salvation from our God and King! Some do not know what they did until

God reveals it to them.

We may have confronted each other and cried out until God reveals the truth. Until then, we are not set free! Check, check and check again. Ask the Lord to reveal if there is any unforgiveness in your heart. If you are seeking for your soul to be content, then forgiveness is a gift. Unwrap that gift and put it to use. Your soul will be freed like a bird!

My soul was once tied up in hatred and sin: anger, resentment, jealousy, self-pity and more. But my Lord and God took hold of me; moment by moment, He revealed the truth that has now set my soul free.

Was it in an instance?
No, not at all.
Oh, I wish it had been done all in one go!

But daily, yearly, every moment of the day - my God showed me His way; how to open up forgiveness like a gift.

Unforgiveness grows all kinds of branches, and bitter roots come from our inability to let go. Some people you needed to forgive are dead and no longer with us. We cannot approach them to say we forgive them, but we can tell our Lord and God that we choose and are happy to forgive. May resentment and bitterness not find refuge inside our souls, for it burdens us more.

Oh, how beautiful it is to forgive others!
My Lord has taught me the importance of forgiveness and also forgetting.

I choose to forgive and to forget all the sins of others from this day

Forgiveness Is a Beautiful Thing!

forth, to love with God's love and help one another. His love does not keep a record of my wrongs, so why should I keep a record of others? Through the blood of Jesus, He has set me free to choose God's ways.

From this time forth, forgiveness and forgetting are who I am! Not through my works but the work of God's Holy Spirit that now lives inside of this body.

It brings light and freedom to praise and worship God in spirit and truth. I will give thanks and praise and worship my God!

How sweet it is to forgive others!

The Lord's unfailing love and mercy still continue,
Fresh as the morning, as sure as the sunrise.

(Lamentations 3:22-23)

CHAPTER TEN

An Empty Room

There is an empty room that was once filled with many possessions. Filled with things of comfort and filled with warmth and love. It was filled with laughter and the sound of grandchildren laughing, crying, and having a good time.

It once contained wardrobes and drawers. They too were filled with all kinds, but the day came when the use of all these items in the room was no longer useful. They had become worn out and old, and the space needed a new refurbishment.

Some grandchildren are now in their 20s, and some are teenagers leading their own lives, the furniture was no longer in much need.

The day came when the clearing out began, but where do we start? Where do we begin? How do we do it? And how do we get rid of the old in the room?

A plan and a vision of what was thought to be after the old had been removed from the room.

The room has been standing for quite a while - needing preparation before the big reveal. There was quite a bit of a mess to start with.

First came the decorator, who stripped the walls bare. Then came the electrician who made a bit of a mess. Along came the plasterer who also made a little bit more mess on the wooden boards; leaving us with a bigger mess to clean up.

Then came in the cleaner - all day it took to clear up the mess from previous workers - one after the other. As I write, the walls are drying out, ready for the next stage, with each process preparing for the final works to come and be done.

The work of the Lord and God can be similar within our hearts as He prepares us for the glory to come: muck, mess and stripping away the old. It feels painful sometimes because our hearts may be stripped naked for the new order of things to be done.

At first, we feel vulnerable and sensitive to everything being stripped away. Some things are no longer useful - our God sometimes strips away right through the nitty - gritty of our souls. We may find ourselves crying out. This cleansing process seems too much, and we are yet to see the final results.

But our God knows exactly what He is doing. He knows the finished results. Many rooms within our hearts are still closed waiting for refurbishment. Our Lord wants us to surrender hearts needing work to Him. He will cleanse every room with His love.

Why do I write about such things? I've learnt that God gives us a deeper understanding at times in everyday occurrences. He needs our cooperation and trust to allow Him to cleanse our hearts; otherwise, the heart becomes covered by worldly things. We try to guard our hearts against pain, for we may have suffered rejection. But our Lord says He came to save. He says He has not rejected you. He loves you and wants to see you healed.

To heal our brokenness and give you a new heart, one of love that pours out for others - a river running through His love - running freely through you for others.

You see, I realised only the other day that through the process of the empty room, the Lord is also doing a new thing deep within my heart. The deeper He goes and makes His home, He has to clear out another room in my heart, so that He can live fully inside this heart. Not in stages, but fully resting and living in my heart. Of course, the flesh wants to resist because the flesh is selfish and wants its own way. It gets comfortable and doesn't like change at all. It familiarises itself and wants to hold onto the old.

But God, through the power of His works within us, can clean out each room as He sees fit. The Holy Spirit teaches the Word of God embedding into the rooms of this heart. For God has something far better after the cleaning has been done.

Now we are waiting for the plumber to fit what is needed in that department. All this so far has taken a while. It will not happen overnight. We've had to be patient while waiting for the next worker. There is the carpet fitter, decorator and new furniture yet to arrive. And then the final assembly of it - all coming together before we can rest, enjoy and see if all the work was worth it!

When Christ first came into our hearts, much needed changing, far more than we ever knew. Unlike our God, who never changes, the empty room has taken on many forms of appearance. But the more profound the relationship, the deeper the cleaning goes on, revealing that things we didn't even know were there at times. We may find it hard to accept that deep within our hearts, we have harboured evil things: jealousy, malice, resentment and despising others for what they are doing.

But the works of God are there to change us and to make us more like Jesus and ready for His coming. The washing of the heart sometimes brings tears when the cleaner comes in to clean up the mess. Not with a mop and bucket, but Words of Truth that cut right through our spirit and soul.

Cleaning is necessary. This, I now understand. And the confession of sins brings forth a cleansing hand. Ah, it may feel as if the job is done, only to find that there is more to come! Unlike us, the cleaner of our heart and soul is at it - 24 hours a day! An 8 - hour shift is enough for us, but the cleaner of our heart never slumbers nor sleeps. He is working with us even as

An Empty Room

the body sleeps.

May this simple writing help us understand God's work within us today!

It has been written in the Word many times. During difficult waiting times, we must discern and avoid being tempted to go to other workers. Wait patiently for the Lord, for we know He will come again.

We must keep asking our God and Father to help us clear up our hearts and souls to submit to God, for He is doing His work for us for our good. To Him be the glory, forever and ever! Our souls are saved for all eternity to live in heaven with our Lord Jesus, our Lord and Saviour.

Now the day has finally arrived when some of the new furnishings have arrived. There is still a way to go, but we can now see that the efforts made have made the transformation journey worthwhile.

After months of planning with, at first, a vision, that vision is beginning to come to fruition. The room has a sense of being brand new; everything in it has been renewed.

The bed has arrived, and we need helpers! The Bible says to ask and receive and the help will come. We need someone to put drawers together and put them up. Finally, the covers and lamps for light will all be placed to make the room a pleasant sight. Clean and fresh bedding with pillows to match will finish off and make the room look much different than before.

As we lay to rest in this room tonight, new beginnings from our Lord above, we are not sure of it all, but we know that our God will not fail us and will guide us through.

It is written in the Word of my God that the end is better than the beginning. We cannot see the finished result, but with our God, in His Word, He gives us insight into what to expect when we are brought home to our Jesus Christ, Our Lord and Saviour. Being made fully in His likeness, we are only a reflection now. May He give us patience in the waiting - as God works within us to prune and shape us. He is preparing us as His bride - spotless and without a wrinkle.

Do not worry about the wrinkles on your face or the body fading like a flower today. Deep inside is beauty within! Be without a spot or wrinkle before finally meeting our bridegroom for all eternity.

May God our Father and Jesus Christ multiply His grace, peace, mercy, love, and truth for you dear friends and readers, brothers and sisters.

To God be the glory for His power at work within us and in the church and Jesus Chris forever and ever!

Amen.

CHAPTER ELEVEN

In Someone Else's Hands

PART ONE

Being Held

Held means to be accountable and responsible for that which we are holding.

When we hold something in our arms or hands, we are responsible for what we do with it. We may be holding something so precious we cannot take our eyes off it. That is how I imagine my God to be; He sees you and me as so special in His sight that he cannot take His eyes off us. He guides, disciplines, and rebukes us at times.

The greatest thing that can happen to us is to be held by God. Even though we can't see His hands, we trust that the Lord embraces us with His mighty hands.

It is written:

"For God loved the world so much that he gave his only Son, so that everyone who believes in him may not die but have eternal life." (John 3:16)

God sent Jesus Christ to save us from all our sins. This means that every sin we commit can be forgiven. It's incredible to think that God had a plan for our salvation even before we were born.

It's a testament to how great and awesome our God truly is.

Our God is a spirit, not a human being. He communicates with us through His Word, the Bible, and the Holy Spirit. These sources teach us the truth about Jesus Christ and the exchange that took place at the cross. By His pure blood, which was never defiled by sin, we can receive redemption and forgiveness for all our sins.

With the guidance of God's Holy Spirit, we can escape the darkness and bask in His divine light. This newfound purpose inspires us to seek a deeper understanding of God and His Son, our Saviour, Jesus Christ.

May our writings serve as a testament to God's glory even after we have left this world. Our actions and stories should remind others that Jesus Christ is on our side, always ready to assist and never standing in our way. No matter where or who we are, He is always eager to hear from us and lend a helping hand.

As you read what has come to be a true testimony of one's personal life, may the Lord God Almighty speak to you and guide you with His hands. The Lord has entrusted my hands to

In Someone's Else's Hand

hold a Chrome Book, take my responsibility seriously and do the work that God has ordained me to do for His Kingdom and its advancement here on earth as it is in heaven. He is the ONE who took hold of me, changed my perspective on life and brought about His perfect will. His love is steadfast and sure; His Holy speaks and teaches only the truth about Jesus Christ, the Son of God.

These writings have become so precious because they glorify Jesus Christ, who gave His life for me because He loves me.

Before we start, let us begin with the prayer that Jesus Christ taught his disciples – derived from the Good News Translation:

> *"Our Father in heaven:*
> *May your holy name be honored;*
> *may your Kingdom come;*
> *may your will be done on earth as it is in heaven.*
> *Give us today the food we need.*
> *Forgive us the wrongs we have done,*
> *as we forgive the wrongs that others have done to us.*
> *Do not bring us to hard testing,*
> *but keep us safe from the Evil One."*
>
> (Matthew 6: 9-13)

PART TWO

Giving Birth

If you have ever given birth or witnessed a child being born, can you remember who was the first person to hold that baby? Usually, it's either the midwife, nurse or even a doctor depending on the situation of the birth.

In normal delivery, as it is called when the baby comes out of the uterus, the midwife is usually there, ready and assisting the baby's head. The baby's head will be held by the midwife responsible for bringing out the baby from its mother's womb. She may pass the baby into someone else's arms, a nurse or doctor. The baby is then held in someone else's arms.

Before the baby is held by its mother, the baby may have been held several times by other people.

This procedure must take place to ensure the baby is breathing well, and that all is OK with the baby. Depending on the circumstances, some babies will be passed on to be held by a specialist nurse in an intensive care unit.

By the time a baby leaves the hospital, several people will have held that baby in their arms and hands. We thank God, the creator of all things, that has made it possible for babies to be delivered safely.

How great is God for His creation of mankind when you think that God, with His eyes, can see that unformed body in its womb and for it to develop into a human being? I do believe God is the creator of all things.

I can remember holding our first child for the first time, looking in amazement and awe that this baby had just emerged from the birth canal. So from the midwife to me, the baby was passed on for me to hold that day.

All the hard work with the labour faded away as my hands held this beautiful baby girl for the first time. Selfishly, I didn't want anyone to look after her, not even her dad. I was committed to feeding her and caring for her every need. It was one of the greatest moments of my life with a deep sense of fulfilment, giving birth to our first child.

Each time my arms held her, my eyes were fixed upon her as I admired her perfect face, eyes, nose, mouth, fingers and toes. I was in awe of such a thing of beauty. It couldn't have grown from just a seed; there had to be a God bigger than we could imagine. However, at the time, I didn't know the Lord as God and Jesus Christ as my Saviour.

I believe now that is how God wants us to be; our eyes fixed upon Him. Our hearts and lives surrendered to Him, for Him to hold. Through Jesus Christ, God has made it possible for us to be made Holy by His Holy Spirit which teaches only truth and cannot lie. Through the cross - where Jesus's hands were pierced with spikes, and through His blood, resurrection and ascension, Jesus is able to hold us now with His righteous and victorious hand and lead us unto God's salvation for eternity to come.

We feel safe in His hand. All fear is cast out through the love of God.

I wanted our daughter to feel safe when held in my arms and loved and wanted. And God loves us with that same love. He wants the best for us and wants us to be the best that we can be while here on earth. He offers us eternal salvation after our outer body dies and returns to the dust.

God's love is limitless! There is no end to His love. It is steadfast and sure. Like a baby in a mother's arms or a responsible person, we feel safe in God's arms and His love. He is gentle and speaks corrections if needed. God disciplines us because He loves us. His Holy Spirit also corrects and leads us into the pureness and true knowledge of Jesus Christ and God the Father.

However, the delivery of our second child was a different story. Although it was a relatively short labour, the birth was harrowing because of the skin tearing as our daughter's head emerged from the birth canal. And by the time the baby was delivered, I was exhausted. Not only that, I had somehow managed to burst some blood vessels in my face through pushing.

When the midwife asked who would like to hold the baby, I answered, "Give her to my husband!" It was the best thing to have done, for at that point, the mother's love had not surfaced within my heart.

Truth be told, I wanted them to take our baby away so I could sleep and get some rest.

Looking back to that day, the nurses must have known. They took our daughter away for the night. Therefore, she would have been held in someone else's arms until they brought her to me the following day.

After a good night's sleep, my love for our second child as my arms took hold of her and feeding came through. Because of the first instinct of not experiencing love immediately, there may have been times when I tried to compensate for that initial moment of no love being there soon after delivery.

God understands everything. He knows all things, and all things are possible with God. With His hand, which is able to exalt, He can mend the most broken – heart, spirit and soul. But that mother's love has never faded for either child. They are now 51 and 47 years of age at the time of publishing,

Although my love doesn't seem as powerful as the one I felt at birth, the love is deeper now. And that's what love does – it grows. We sometimes think our love has gone for the people we care for in our lives, but that love is demonstrated in what we do for them.

Hallelujah!

Praise the Lord, for He is good. His love endures forever.

                                                       Amen.

But the most beautiful moment of being held is knowing that we have a loving Saviour who is able to hold us in His hand. Although our physical eyes may not see, our hearts can feel and sense that our Lord Jesus Christ is holding us by His righteous right hand. The Lord makes me dwell in safety when I lay down to sleep. I've learnt to lay down, surrender, and listen to what God says, speaking His Word and truth.

Praise the Lord, for He is good! His mercy endures forever.

Amen.

PART THREE

Hands that Hold

When we look at hands, we see four fingers and one thumb on each. Some may have fingers missing; others may not have hands, yet they find ways of holding things. These hands do a lot, from creativity with art, sewing, cooking and cleaning. There are hands which cut our hair and make clothes for us to wear—so many functions beyond the scope of these writings.

Hands can bring comfort. A gentle touch on someone's back can say I LOVE YOU. The same hands can transfer compassion. However, hands can also be used to transfer someone's hate. Then there are the good hands that fed us as children and maybe still make meals for us in our old age.

But the greatest hands of all that can hold us belong to the Lord. In the Book of Isaiah, it is written:

"But you, Israel my servant,
you are the people that I have chosen,

In Someone Else's Hand

the descendants of Abraham, my friend.
I brought you from the ends of the earth;
I called you from its farthest corners and said to you,
'You are my servant.' I did not reject you, but chose you.
Do not be afraid—I am with you!

I am your God—let nothing terrify you!
I will make you strong and help you;
I will protect you and save you.

"Those who are angry with you will know the shame of defeat.
Those who fight against you
will die and will disappear from the earth.
I am the Lord your God; I strengthen you and tell you,
'Do not be afraid; I will help you.'"

The Lord says,

"Small and weak as you are, Israel,
don't be afraid; I will help you.
I, the holy God of Israel, am the one who saves you.
I will make you like a threshing board,
with spikes that are new and sharp.
You will thresh mountains and destroy them;
hills will crumble into dust.
You will toss them in the air; the wind will carry them off,
and they will be scattered by the storm.

Then you will be happy because I am your God;
you will praise me, the holy God of Israel."

(Isaiah 41:8-16)

Precious in His Sight

This piece of Scripture caused my inner being and relationship with God to be changed. It was as if God was revealing who He is as Lord and God, my Redeemer and the Holy One of Israel. He encouraged me not to be afraid, saying, "Do not be afraid; I will help you." He assured me that all my enemies who hate me would be led to confusion and humiliation.

Who are our enemies? Ignorance of **who** and **what** Christ did is an enemy, and so is lust, lying, jealousy, and the unbelief of Christ and what he did. The issues we face against God's will for our lives are also our enemies, not forgetting the devil and all His accomplishes who he uses to try and derail us from God's truth. But the two main agents Satan uses are self-pity and resentment.

Satan is defeated by the blood of Jesus and what Jesus did on the cross. The work at the cross was perfect. It may not have looked perfect with the visible eye, and it would have been horrific to watch, but the spiritual victory was and is perfect.

I remember when I used to do some voluntary at a hospital. One day, I was feeling unhappy, feeling a deep pain inside and mentally dejected. I didn't know why, for I knew I desired to know God and do His will. I knew that the work at the hospital was good. I asked a question, "Lord, what is this about?"

The answer was quite surprising; that still, small and gentle voice said, "It is self-pity."

Now, I didn't know how to be relieved from self-pity as it

had become part of my sinful nature whenever things didn't turn out how I would have liked. Although I was trying my best, self-pity reared its ugly head once in a while. It would drag me down such that it became difficult to envision where God was leading me to go. But praise the Lord and God, who is wise. Gradually, He began to teach me and show me the truth until I was completely delivered from self-pity.

One of the first reactions in the process of deliverance was to ask God if there was anyone I hadn't forgiven. I also told the Lord that I was willing to forgive. I chose forgiveness because He had forgiven me for all my iniquities. How can your sins be forgiven if you don't forgive others?

He is our Lord and God of Israel, The Holy One of Israel, The Alpha and Omega, The author and finisher of this faith! To Him who is able to keep us from stumbling and make our spirit whole, preserving body and soul and keeping us in His blameless love for the day of our Lord Jesus Christ's coming.

To Him be the glory forever and ever!

You see, at times in our lives, we need to know the hand holding us. The Lord keeps me in His righteous and victorious hand. Each morning, there is a process of yielding; a time to surrender and allow my God to speak of His Word to strengthen me once more.

When you take time to read and study the Bible, His living Word becomes like a river flowing through us to give us life and uphold us. The Holy Spirit has a way of opening us up spiritually as we find strength. His love envelopes us. We feel lighter and more peaceful inside. If God is for us, then who can be against us?

Glory to the Holy One of Israel, God the creator and eternal God!

PART FOUR

Now in the Hand of The Lord My God: A Word of Praise!

By the time you read this book, dear reader, understand that I would have gone through many moments of being led and guided by His hands. The work would have diligently gone through other hands who will help bring forth the writings inspired by the ONE who now holds me and will carry me to eternal life with Him.

May the Lord my God make a way, even through internet connections, to bring the writings to those waiting to hear about God the Father, Jesus Christ, His Son and the Holy Spirit. All three are one. The Holy Trinity works together, working ALL things together for God's purpose for others.

I believe God has taken hold of me. He holds me in His righteous and victorious hand - my God has taken hold of me. This life belongs to Him. My spirit, soul and body now all belong to

God. That includes every cell, tissue and fibre of my being, mind and heart! For through Jesus Christ and the perfect work and exchange at the cross, the blood of Jesus sanctifies us, making all things possible with God.

The ONE who made me and made a life as I stand committed to doing the will of God. My King, who I will serve before it is time for my spirit and soul to leave this earthly vessel. He holds this tongue, lips and mouth to confess that Jesus Christ is alive and seated with my God at His side. The blood of Jesus is speaking even now out in heaven for you and me. Being able to serve others is an honour and privilege; following the steps of Jesus Christ and His disciples. His love flows through His people for all peoples of the nations.

In your arms, you now hold me, Lord, and my God.

Thank You, Jesus, for revealing that your Father is the only true God.

You have made my heart glad more than at any other time. You have turned my mourning into dancing, taken off my sackcloth and given me the oil of joy instead of sorrow. You have given me a garment of praise instead of a spirit of heaviness.

You have made my hands holy that they may be lifted, rejoicing and waving to you, my King. I believe you can see the hands you have created lifted up toward heaven, praising you, my God and King. Your Word is working and has transformed from within; a heart and mind for you, my King. A purpose-driven life to know my God, to walk and function in His love, to trust and obey the Word of God.

> One Lord.
>
> One faith.
>
> One God.
>
> One baptism.
>
> One Holy Spirit of God.

Glory to God forever for His everlasting love and mercy He has shown me! Saved by His Grace, He causes me to be purified by confessing the Word of God.

Now these writings I place in your hands, my Lord and God, for you to do your will with them as you see fit, Oh, righteous Father and Holy God!

In the name of Jesus, bless the diligent work of the hands working on these writings. May you add no sorrow to the work of their hands. Share with them what you would have done for me, Lord and God Almighty. That others will know of your greatness, Oh Lord! And that these writings would feed your sheep, dear Lord.

May those who don't know which way to go hear your voice as you speak to them clearly about your love. Lead and guide them so that no one would be lost.

In Someone Else's Hand

Now to you, Oh Righteous and Holy God!
To you be the glory forever and ever.

Amen.

✝

Even if I go through the deepest darkness,
I will not be afraid, Lord, for you are with me.
Your shepherd's rod and staff protect me.

(Psalm 23:4)

CHAPTER TWELVE

In the Valley and On the Mountain

You are there when we are in the valley of decision and indecision!
When we are on the mountains of pain and confusion,
Lord, you are there.

My Lord and God, you are there.
In times of trouble, you are there.
The blood of Jesus washes us through to make us whole.

Through the blood of Jesus, He has redeemed us and
brought us into His kingdom of light.
That even in the valley, He is with us.
As we go deep, He is there to meet us!
He speaks the truth and not lies.
He feeds us.
In the valley of judgment, He disciplines and corrects us.

Our Lord is HOLY; everything He does is sacred.
He has covered us in Christ Jesus through His blood.

Precious in His Sight

Holiness and righteousness are ours by grace.

The Lord has promised never to leave or forsake us.
He is a Promise Keeper and will come again to save and
bring us home into eternal life with our Lord and God.

For the God who is the creator and created all things;
He has got hold of me and will not let me go.

Keep self-pity away from me, our Lord!
Remove any roots that they bear no more fruit,
Even in my old age, Lord.
Because of you, my Lord and God,
your pearl of the prize will bear good fruit.

The fruit of patience, kindness, and a pure and clean heart.

Thank you for pen and paper, Dear Lord.
Praise Your Holy Name!
Praise you, for allowing me to offload to you, Dear Lord.

CHAPTER THIRTEEN

Are We There Yet?

Introduction

Have you ever found yourself pondering as you journey through life... are we there yet in our spiritual quest?

When we are on a journey, there is a specific route that we may need to take to get to the destination we are heading for.

We may need a map, or nowadays, we use Google Maps. Before, it was a physical map book that we picked up and read and planned out our routes. After that came the Sat Nav, which we placed in the car charger and the instructions were given by someone's voice in the machine.

But now we have many other types of software in cars or phones to guide us to our destinations. A man's or woman's voice speaks out the roads we need to take and the lanes we need to be in if we are on the A-roads or motorways: instructing us to go left or right, first exit, second exit, third exit, and so on at the roundabouts.

My husband of 51 years still enjoys looking at a physical map as he drives. He memorises landmarks to help him determine where he is on the journey. What works better for me is marking down the road numbers. As the route is set out, the road numbers are written on an A4 sheet of paper. The exits of any roundabout are written down as the first, second, or third exit.

If there are any lanes to change, the road numbers are usually written on the roads in England. Thanks be to God for the nation of England. Still, whether it's a short or long journey, children often ask, "Are we there yet?"

When Jesus Christ first called me to follow Him, I didn't realise it would be a journey. I was unaware that the journey of faith would become a lifetime journey of discovering who God is, who Jesus is and why God sent Him into this world long before I was born. He came to be crucified upon a cross, carrying all my sins and everyone else's upon Himself to the cross. That the blood of Jesus would wash our sins, sanctify and justify us marvellously and wonderfully by faith.

When I first started following Jesus Christ, I didn't fully comprehend that I would need to search and study the Bible. Lessons and stories reveal the truth of who God is, who the Son of God is, and what the Holy Spirit of God does to help and teach us the truth of Christ Jesus.

Are We There Yet?

Like a reliable map or a satellite navigation system on a motorway, the Bible provides clear instructions to walk truthfully toward our ultimate destination, heaven.

The journey of faith in Christ is believing in something we have not yet seen, yet we love Him even though we have never seen Him. We learn to trust deeply with respect.

We believe that there is a life eternal with Him and that when we see Him one day, we will become just like Him. The Holy Spirit, our divine guide, helps us evolve in His likeness. It helps us reflect on the errors of our ways. We come to hate what we used to like before. We now hate what we used to do as we are woken up to the fact that we are sinners, how grave sin is, and its effect on our lives.

All glory be to God the Father and Jesus Christ for His mercy and grace - bestowed upon us and save us from eternal death.

Back to the question, "Are we there yet?" The answer is NOT YET.

We are still alive and living in the land of the living; we haven't arrived yet at our eternal destination.

We are still travelling on the journey to eternal life by faith, not by what we see with our human eyes, but by listening with an internal ear to what the Spirit of the Church of our Lord and God is saying.

God has opened up our ears in a spiritual way so that we can hear what His Holy Spirit is saying. We have a Book of all kinds of help and skills to keep us on the right path. When I started my faith journey in 2003, I walked through a church building's doors, and a pastor gave me a book titled *The Bible*.

As young children, we attended Sunday schools, where we were told about Jesus and shown pictures of Him on a cross.

But we were never told why He was crucified. I must have been around nine or ten when I heard a voice clearly speaking in my ear and saying, "Follow me." At the time, I was hanging up my coat in the school cloakroom one day. I felt peace that day, a certain kind of peace which lasted for about two weeks.

But I didn't know who had spoken those words; there was no one to confide in or ask questions.

But as I write this in 2021, there is no doubt in my mind, heart and soul that Jesus Christ called me to follow Him as a young child.

There have been many days when I regretted not following Him earlier, other than a two-week stint, but God's Word tells me that a thousand years are like one day to Him. Although it took until 2003 to finally begin to follow Christ Jesus seriously, that day He called me in the cloakroom is still the day of the Lord.

I believe that God's time is not like worldly time. God may not work in weeks, months and years. Therefore, wherever you are and however long you have been on the journey with Christ

Jesus, it is the same day of the Lord as He called you, despite what the earthly calendar says. This means that every day is an opportunity to walk in His light and follow His path, regardless of how long we've been on this journey.

Now let us consider that to be GOOD NEWS!

May these writings encourage you wherever you are on your journey. God is a God of hope. When all hope seems lost, God is so powerful that He can bring us out of the bottomless, darkest pit.

These writings are of the journey with Jesus Christ at the ship's helm, guiding us into safer waters. The truth is written of the trip so far: pit stops, times to stop and refuel and times of rejoicing when a breakthrough has come. I rely on God the Father, Jesus Christ and the Holy Spirit to navigate us to the final destination.

Are we there yet?

The answer is not yet, but we are steadily making progress on our journey!

The Reason

For every journey we may take, there is a reason why we are to travel on the trip. There is always a reason why we would like to go on that journey.

Let us take, for instance, a relative who is in the hospital and not well. We would want to do all we can to help that relative in their time of trouble, hoping to comfort them and reassure them that they will get well.

What do we say?

What do we take?

How will we get there?

Words are powerful, and what we say can make a difference to the one we speak to. What we take may depend upon the person's likes. How we get there will depend on the mode of transport. The body is a vehicle in itself.

I believe God created man, not just man but all creation. The body and its systems are a miraculous and marvellous piece of engineering designed by God himself. I believe God has created heaven and earth, and I believe God is making right now a new heaven, a new Jerusalem that He will bring out of the clouds one day for His people to live in.

Now we are born, and yet we shall die too.

I believe no one is born by mistake in God's sight, and we are all given the gift of life for a reason. With God, it is for a specific reason.

Life here on earth will never be without suffering, for our world is not perfect. But if God is for us, then who can be against us? If we have been joined to the Spirit of Jesus Christ, the love of

Christ is in us, the Love of the Father holds us, and He gives us a reason to commit our lives to Him.

We were created to live, love all people, help who we can when we can, and do what we can to help others.

Oh, there are times when I have thought I could change the world! But if we change as individuals and people, the world will change.

Hearts need to be changed, for even God says that man's heart is wicked. Until God reveals to us the depths of our hearts, we do not know what is in them.

God created us to be like Him, to love, and to live a good life with unconditional love, never wavering, not arguing, not being jealous of others, always forgiving, and doing what is right in God's sight. God had a relationship with Adam, to begin with, until Adam ate the apple from the Tree of Knowledge, and sin came into the world and separated man from God.

God told Adam not to eat fruit from the Tree of Knowledge because God knew the consequences of doing so. But Satan deceived Eve into thinking it was OK to eat the forbidden fruit, and she'd share it with Adam.

However, God came up with an even greater plan. He sent His Begotten Son, Jesus Christ, into the world. The reason was for our salvation. God planned to reconcile man back to himself as it was before sin entered into the world and defiled what God had created for good.

There are reasons why we all do things: think about what we do, say what we say and react the way we do. There is a reason for every action.

For example, what was the reason men and women were made? So that children can be reproduced. The Bible says God blessed Adam and Eve and said,

> *"Have many children so that your descendants will live*
> *all over the earth and bring it under their control.*
> *I am putting you in charge of the fish, the birds, and*
> *all the wild animals."* (Genesis 1:28)

Who can fathom God's mind? Who can fathom God's thoughts? None of us can unless God gives us insight and revelations into what He has done and continues to do in our lives.

Man is at God's mercy, for He sees into the depths of our hearts. We cannot get away from anything or hide from God. We cannot hide what we have done wrong from God. He has eyes to see the depth of a man's heart and soul. We may have hidden it from our families, but with God, it is impossible to hide anything from Him.

Still, God sent Jesus Christ, His Son, so that He would carry all our sins, sorrows, griefs, sickness and disease, shame, guilt, doubts and fears, self-pity and resentment, lies and deceit. The list goes on and on.

If we invite Jesus Christ as our Lord and Saviour with all our hearts and accept Jesus Christ to come and live in our hearts, we will be set upon a journey. It is not visible with the human eyes but can be known by faith within the depths of our being.

We have to be given the gift of faith to believe that the faith God gives us will be why we will live the rest of our lives committed to God through Jesus Christ. God will put us right with Him. He will end sins' power over us so that when temptation comes, God will show us how to resist and walk away from that temptation.

The Holy Spirit helps us become a reflection of Jesus until the day of salvation when we will see the fullness of who we are in Christ.

We encourage others to give their lives to Jesus for many reasons. He is the only way to live right and peacefully beyond human understanding. Jesus came for the lost and for those who know they are sinners.

The very reason why these writings are taking place is because Jesus called me, and by God's gift of grace, He came to save me. Why?

So that I may receive eternal life in heaven once the body passes away.

So many reasons lead to other reasons why we need a relationship with God! Remember, God gave us Jesus Christ so that we might love and treat others as He loved us. He showed us His love and forgiveness through Jesus Christ.

The Preparation

Now, with all journeys, one needs to PREPARE. Preparing in advance helps us deal with any unforeseen circumstances while travelling. I remember many years ago when our family travelled to Majorca. Now, we had never travelled abroad before or even flown!

So, preparations had to be made. We needed passports to enter another country. We required suitable clothing and footwear as the weather was far hotter than we were used to in England. We also required sun creams so our skin wouldn't burn due to the excess exposure.

Many items were placed in the suitcase: mosquito repellent, sun creams, sandals, delicate linen dresses, swimwear and towels for the beach.

We had passports and tickets ready to be accepted on the flight and made transport arrangements to get to the airport. Five children, aged eighteen months to ten years old, were present. A pushchair, nappies, and all needed to look after an eighteen-month-old child was at hand.

The children were excellent as we travelled the one-and-a-half-hour journey to Manchester airport. As we approached and entered the terminal, people were there to help us make sure we had checked in the right way. All seemed to be going smoothly.

Then, suddenly, there was an announcement that our flight

had been delayed for several hours.

Now, that wasn't something we had prepared for! It was all new to us, but to those well-travelled, they had experienced it before. So those who had experienced delays before reassured us it was something that could happen. If I had gone through those delays today, there would have been prayers of thanksgiving and praise rather than disappointment. But this happened when I didn't know Jesus Christ as Lord and Saviour.

We did not anticipate delays; the airline we flew with only let us know once we got to the airport. The delay lasted for a few hours. Fortunately, we were at Manchester airport, and the English currency brought us food and drink.

When I think of these things, I think of Jesus Christ coming again. God has given us His Word in the Bible and tells us that He will send Jesus Christ again—for the church to be handed over to God. As Christians, we believe that we will be able to share in God's glory once we receive our resurrected bodies in the new heavens and the new earth. We will experience a deeper connection with our Creator and will no longer be at risk of falling into sin. God's glory will be everything to us, and we will be completely immersed in it.

The Holy Spirit works in us beyond our complete understanding and, at times, helps us prepare for the day when we meet with our God and King, our Lord and Saviour.

The Destination

The first time we flew, our destination was Majorca, and we safely arrived in the latter hours that day. We spent ten days with our young family in the warm sunshine before setting off once more to travel back to England.

We were not prepared for what was to come yet again on our return. When we arrived at the airport and headed for the terminal, we only had a few passatas left in currency at the time. Once more, there was a call on the loudspeaker of an unexpected delay back to England.

We had not prepared drinks and food for the five-hour delay, and the money we had left was enough to buy one Mars bar – not enough to share amongst nine of us. We each had a bite, and that was it! My heartfelt despondent and disappointment again. I had not expected another delay back home, let alone prepared for it.

However, we eventually arrived safely back in the UK.

From that time on, wherever we go, I ensure we have enough money or food packed for any unforeseen delays. Of course, things have changed, and we now have debit cards to pay for most items.

But what about our final destination after we die? Once this body of flesh has passed away, what about that destination?

Do we ever think: Are We There Yet?

Sometimes, we may think we have arrived, especially after a significant achievement. However, the Bible assures us that our ultimate destination is heaven, where we will behold Jesus Christ and become like Him.

In the meantime, the Holy Spirit of God is working within us, helping us to live in a way that reflects Christ's character.

Conclusion

At the present moment, we are all work in progress. We are all foreigners in this world. We have become foreigners on earth because of what God has done for us. Our final destination is heaven, where we can live in the new Jerusalem.

And through the cross and Jesus Christ, God himself has made us overcome the world.

Do not cling to events of the past
or dwell on what happened long ago.

Watch for the new thing I am going to do.
It is happening already—you can see it now!
I will make a road through the wilderness
and give you streams of water there.

(Isaiah 43:18-19)

CHAPTER FOURTEEN

No Turning Back

The concept of not turning back has been on my mind, and I have considered the Lord's Word. According to Scripture, His disciples were not supposed to look back. The Lord also instructs us to pick up our cross, a wise saying from our Lord and God.

However, stopping our minds from dwelling on unpleasant experiences can be challenging. Luckily, the Lord assures us that we can cast our burdens onto Him, and He will give us rest for our souls.

I remember times when I prayed, and the Lord quickly answered my request. Other times, it's taken longer for painful memories to fade. Forgiveness has been the key to experiencing freedom from my burdens. It's like our God is a rubber erasing those painful memories as I cast my burdens onto Him, choosing to forgive those who hurt me.

I believe anything is possible for God. I know the many

Precious in His Sight

painful memories He has helped me forget through prayer. Sometimes, these memories resurface, almost like watching them on a TV screen. But through these moments of weakness, I have learned the power of forgiveness and releasing painful thoughts and visions to the Lord. I share my experiences not to deceive anyone but to offer hope to those struggling. If you have a memory that continues to haunt you, know that the Lord can take it away.

Sometimes, confronting the consequences of a past event, even if it happened many years ago, takes time. The pain from that event may still be buried deep within us, and we may hesitate to face it. But we can work through our grief and find healing with patience, self-care and faith.

Did you experience abuse or trauma that affected your childhood? Did something happen to you, the kind of event or occurrence you still carry, no matter how many times you try to forget? Many people have gone through painful circumstances now etched within their memories - resurfacing once every while to torment us further. However, I firmly believe that only the Lord can heal such wounds completely. He possesses the ability to see what humans cannot see, hear what they cannot, and heal our damaged souls with His touch.

Our Lord Jesus Christ offers comforting advice to go to Him so we can find rest for our souls. The Bible says,

> *"Come to me, all you who are weary and burdened, and I will give you rest. Take my yoke upon you and*

> *learn from me, for I am gentle and humble in heart,*
> *and you will find rest for your souls.*
> *For my yoke is easy and my burden is light."*
>
> (Matthew 11:28-30)

Painful memories keep us in darkness and prevent us from experiencing what God desires us to know, feel and experience as His children. You may remember when your prayers were answered and experienced mighty breakthroughs. However, your current and future circumstances might be dealt with in ways you never knew because He is God. Don't limit His power based on your limited understanding of who He is and what He can do.

> *"But the Lord says, Do not cling to events of the past or*
> *dwell on what happened long ago. Watch for the new thing*
> *I am going to do. It is happening already—you can see it now!*
> *I will make a road through the wilderness and give you*
> *streams of water there."* (Isaiah 43:18-19)

These words are meant to guide us and will not go void, for they are the ultimate truth. It's up to us to heed and unburden our souls, surrendering all we are for complete healing. These words of wisdom come from the ONE who possesses all the knowledge we will ever need.

Jesus is a wonderful friend who heals and delivers my soul!

I bless the Lord with all my heart and soul, for He has set me free like a bird. I am at peace because the Lord has been generous to me.

We need to reach a point where we trust in the Author and Finisher of our faith and look forward. Let us not dwell on the past and allow Him to guide us towards our destiny.

CHAPTER FIFTEEN

Plans to Prosper

The Book of Jeremiah in the Bible teaches us that God's plans for us are always good and not meant to harm us. His thoughts towards us are thoughts of peace. The scripture also tells us that God's thoughts are not like ours, and His ways are not ours. Therefore, in our old age, we may find ourselves doing things we did not anticipate.

Walking with Jesus Christ, He takes us to places we could not have imagined. This journey becomes steps of faith. It's exciting at times, for our Lord and God has assured us that His plans are meant for good and not bring harm or struggles.

So, if the next step you are about to take has been ordered by our God, do not lean on your own understanding. Instead, submit to the Lord, who will lead you on a level path. He will straighten the way for you and lead you on the right path.

There are times when it seems we are pushing so hard for a

door to open; those times when door after door is being shut. It may be a sign that the Lord does not want you to go to those places anymore. No one can fathom His understanding or how great He is! All we can do is learn to trust in our God and King. How do we do that when things seem to be out of control? Go to His Word and ask the Lord what He is saying about your uncomfortable situation.

Ask the Lord to speak to your heart as you read the Bible. Dear friends, keep searching until you find a piece of scripture that speaks directly to your soul and spirit. Then, ask God to show you where He wants you to go or what to do. It may take a while, or the answer might require you to spend some time in the presence of the Lord.

He will lift you when you humble yourself and surrender your burdens to the Lord God Almighty. Only our God knows the answers to all the questions we seek, not other people who might not understand how the Lord works in our lives as individuals. All I can do as a writer is encourage you to look unto Jesus Christ, who was the Word, became the Word and is the Word—the one who can help you on your way and be your guide.

Don't give up, dearest reader! Keep pressing in and on, for Christ is our Healer. He heals your mind, body and soul. He was wounded that we may be healed, pierced that we may be forgiven, punished that we may receive His peace, cursed that we may be blessed and made poor that we may be rich. When we talk about His riches, we refer to the richness of the treasures from

His Word. These include peace, forgiveness, wisdom, understanding, healing, and wholeness. Everything good comes from our Lord and God.

I was once buried alive, not being able to see the way out of that darkest place. I was vulnerable, unstable and broken, and He heard my cry from the depths of that scene and took hold of me with His victorious right hand. He pulled me out of the darkest tomb - buried alive inside a body.

He placed within this body His Holy Spirit, who began to teach the truth from that day. It set me free; that is the case to this day.

But I once was stuck in the wilderness, tempted by the devil, crying, 'Where are you, Oh God?" And yet, He was right by my side - encouraging me. I found myself on my face day after day, repenting and realising that I was a sinner. It took the power of the Holy Spirit to reveal the depths of my sins. But all along, God's plan has always been greater: to cleanse this body of sin so that I could walk in a manner that is worthy and fully pleasing to the Lord, to bear good fruit in every good work.

God is worthy of all thanksgiving, praise, and worship! May we stand when our Lord stands, walk when He walks, sit with Him daily, and listen to His heart.

If God is for us, then who can be against us? What God has joined together, let no one separate them. It is written,

> *"For I am certain that nothing can separate us from his love: neither death nor life, neither angels nor other heavenly rulers or powers, neither the present nor the future, neither the world above nor the world below—there is nothing in all creation that will ever be able to separate us from the love of God which is ours through Christ Jesus our Lord."*
>
> (Romans 8:38-39)

Through the cross, the blood, and Jesus Christ, we can receive a new regeneration of life in Christ and a healed heart. We receive a spirit that is whole and willing to yield to our Lord and God for the power of His works of salvation within us. We serve others as God's servants here on earth until we are called home and our work is done.

CHAPTER SIXTEEN

He Who Calms the Storm
A Cry For Help – Penned During a Medical Predicament

When trials come and the unexpected shows up, we find reassurance in the Lord, our refuge, who calms the storm within. There is a place of solace where we can turn to Him, the one who calms the storm.

The Lord, our constant companion, guides and advocates for us through His Holy Spirit. He reassures us with His truth and reminds us of His unwavering promises. In His boundless mercy, the Lord has guided me through every trial and test, providing comfort and strength.

Crying out helps us pass the tests. Oh, Lord our God! Help us during this trial so that we may rejoice in you. Oh Lord our God, you have promised never to leave or forsake us.

I stand in the waiting room for our call, many people looking sad and lost. Pain on their faces - heads spinning, trying to make sense of it all. I find myself digging deep to seek His peace as we wait for someone to call our names. There's hope that the treatment will come soon to relieve a relative from all their pain.

Calm on the outside but paddling inside, clinging to the Word of God - words He has spoken in the secret place.

Several hours pass, talking to other visitors and passers-by. Some will never be seen again, yet the Lord is with us and helping us all. Finally, the nurse explains and instructs us where we must go. Off we travel—to the next port of call, the right place for treatment to bring health once more.

At last, we return to the quiet place - the inward secret refuge which gives solace to the soul. I lay down and listen to what our Lord and Saviour has to say about the situation.

Home alone and yet never alone, for my Lord has walked amongst us all day.

A warm meal and a shower and a bed to rest our heads.

All will be much different in the morning as the day breaks.

I am reminded about what the Lord says,

> *"Come, everyone who is thirsty — here is water!*
> *Come, you that have no money — buy corn and eat!*
> *Come! Buy wine and milk — it will cost you nothing!"*
> (Isiah 51:1)

Being still and listening intently with the inner ear, the storm once more calms within me. Jesus, again and again, calms the storm within me. Human weaknesses depend upon our Lord and God.

As dawn breaks, there's thanksgiving in my heart, for my Lord and Saviour has shown His perfect strength once more. "Do not be afraid, do not fear!" are always the words from my Saviour. I can sense Him saying, "I will uphold you with my right and victorious hand. I will strengthen you and help you. I, the Lord myself, will help you."

Oh! How we need to give God thanks all the time!

His promise comes true each and every time.

He knows our weaknesses, and that's OK.

Even in our shortcomings, He always shows us His perfect love and strength.

Forever grateful, forever thankful to my Lord and Saviour for saving me!

He has washed, comforted, encouraged and fed me. How do we describe the goodness of our God?

Mercy.
Grace.
Peace.

Love and truth that reveals who we belong to.

For He has brought us out of darkness into the light.

Precious in His Sight

We need to understand that we have a Holy Father who will discipline and correct us, prune and feed us, and continue to love us. One day, our Lord and Saviour will take us to our heavenly home to live forever and sing glory to our King!

Take heart, my friends. Do not waver in your faith. Keep pushing forward, for the Holy Spirit will not allow you to falter. Do not boast in your triumphs, but rejoice in Jesus Christ! He conquers every evil and wickedness, enabling us to lead a Righteous life that pleases our God.

Are there disappointments?

Take them to the Lord. Do we feel God has heard our prayers at all? Are we asking out of selfish need? Let us check how we pray so that our prayers will succeed. And when we ask, BELIEVE that your prayers have been answered.

For it is written,

> *"I assure you that whoever tells this hill to get up and throw itself in the sea and does not doubt in his heart, but believes that what he says will happen, it will be done for him. For this reason I tell you: When you pray and ask for something, believe that you have received it, and you will be given whatever you ask for."*
>
> (Mark 11:23-24)

Our Father in heaven answers our calls in the name of Jesus Christ and bring forth here on earth the prayer that we asked, even for the salvation of the whole household.

He Who Calms the Storm

Who is able to calm the storm within?

Only Jesus Christ, our Lord and Saviour! Glory be to Him forever.

Where does my help come from?

It comes from the Lord!

Amen.

Try to be at peace with everyone, and try to live a holy life, because no one will see the Lord without it. Guard against turning back from the grace of God. Let no one become like a bitter plant that grows up and causes many troubles with its poison.

(Isaiah 43:18-19)

CHAPTER SEVENTEEN

Time to Eat Meat

The time has come to eat meat and continue with the vegetables. No, I'm not talking about beef and carrots, but the Word of God.

When we eat meat, it takes some time to digest and reach our intestines. However, once it does, it can help us release negative emotions like lies and anger, reducing our urge to fight. Ultimately, we will realise that we genuinely need the essence of the Word - the Bible, rather than being tossed around like a baby in the waves of the sea.

This meat nourishes and strengthens our souls to find rest and deal with others the way God intended, the way Jesus Christ taught us.

Dear friends and readers, there will be times when frustration and anger arise. In those moments, I've learnt to ask the Lord for help, for fretting only leads to sin. Now the meat of the

Word tells me that I cannot keep sinning if I am in Christ. And so, I chew on that Word, contemplating what it truly means, hoping that the Holy Spirit of my God will help me apply it deep within my soul.

As we journey with Christ, our Lord and the Holy Spirit, we learn to become more like God while on earth. The idea of being accountable to God for every careless word reminds me to be mindful of my speech. I am grateful for Jesus Christ, who, through the Holy Spirit, fills my mouth with positive words.

The meat also reminds me of any confessions to be cleansed and purified again through Jesus Christ, the Great High Priest. Like a child, we sometimes need to ask our heavenly Father for His advice and guidance on all life matters.

I remember how not too long ago, we had to make travel arrangements for a church trip. There were moments of frustration, anxiety and feeling misunderstood. But as I reflect on what was going on, I now realise that I needed to ponder on the meat of the Word of God. I should have asked my Father in Heaven, Jesus Christ, my Lord and Saviour and the Holy Spirit for advice on which bus company to use.

The flesh opposes the spirit, and the sinful nature sometimes opposes the goodness of the Holy Spirit, but the Holy Spirit is far more powerful and superior. And so, we declare that greater is He that is within than in the world.

What do we say then about the meat of the Word? It is crucial because our Lord God Almighty will test our faith. It is written that faith will be tested and refined like gold:

> *"These have come so that the proven genuineness of your faith—of greater worth than gold, which perishes even though refined by fire—may result in praise, glory and honour when Jesus Christ is revealed."*
>
> (1 Peter 1:7)

The teachings of God's Word reveal the truth and do not deceive us. They help us discover our true selves in Christ and eliminate our old ways.

How great is our God! His greatness is much more than we can fathom.

It is crucial not to compromise the gospel, as it is only through Christ Jesus that we can be liberated from sin permanently. By gaining knowledge and using the Word, we can triumph over the many challenges that come our way, such as our old selves and the devil's lies. Additionally, it is necessary to exercise discernment, particularly during moments of purification. It is crucial to differentiate between God's voice, and the enemy's during these difficult times of cleansing. The voice you listen to is critical.

Sometimes it may feel like punishment, but God gives us the necessary strength to get through it. Although we cannot fully comprehend the suffering of Jesus Christ, the teachings of the

Bible suggest that if we have been crucified with Him, we will also be resurrected with Him.

When we humbly surrender to God's will and authority, we come to the profound realisation that as sinners, we need the deeper truths and teachings of God's Word. With joy and inner peace, we are empowered to go out, spreading the good news with our feet adorned by the gospel, and our journey made beautiful as we descend from the mountain.

Let's strive to connect with God and fully immerse ourselves in His teachings. Our salvation solely depends on God; only He can provide us with true joy and happiness.

Let's consume the valuable knowledge He offers to strengthen our faith.

CHAPTER EIGHTEEN

In the Procession

The Word of our God states that we are in a great procession with our Lord, Jesus Christ, Our Saviour who has already gone before us and won every victory for us. No one can fathom the greatness of God, and no one can understand all of His ways. Still, His Word tells us what Christ achieved on the cross. It is written,

> *"And on that cross, Christ freed himself from the power of the spiritual rulers and authorities; he made a public spectacle of them by leading them as captives in His victory procession."* (Colossians 2:15)

God has given us the spirit of faith; that we may believe that He loves us so much that He sent His Son to be crucified for all our sins. He raised Jesus Christ from the grave so that we might live through Him. By faith, we are washed, sanctified, justified and forgiven of all our sins. Through His blood, we are more than conquerors, not victims of whatever life throws at us.

Precious in His Sight

Our God is not a God of confusion! With His love, He can bring light and clarity to any situation and heal our hearts. In His everlasting love, He carries us forth in His arms. At times, it feels like we have to dig deeper to find the treasures of our God and King. May they fall gently into our hearts today. Just one touch from our Lord and King brings relief from the world of sin.

Through Christ, we have been set free from every sin. The Bible teaches us that by His grace, which abounds more than our sin, we can overcome our sins and receive forgiveness and cleansing of unrighteousness from the Most High Priest, Jesus Christ. Through His precious blood, He has cleansed us and set us apart for God. We serve Him and are made righteous and Holy through Him.

Of course, we dare not say that there is no sin in these fleshly bodies today, but God's Word tells me that by His grace, God has put an end to the power of sin over us. Progressive sanctification is in motion today – regenerating believers to overcome sin – living and loving like Christ.

Jesus warned us there would be many trials and temptations. Therefore, we must stay on guard and never give up praying. There will be false teachers and prophets trying to deceive us. Let us pray and ask God to grant us spiritual discernment to know who lives by the truth so that we may not be led astray.

Are you anxious today?

Is your heart troubled today?

In the Procession

Here's what Jesus said,

> *"Don't worry about anything but in all your prayers ask God for what you need, always asking him with a thankful heart. And God's peace, which is far beyond human understanding, will keep your hearts and minds safe in union with Christ Jesus."*
>
> (Philippians 4:6-7)

How do we walk with our Lord?

Not through our own strength and effort, by the power of God's Spirit.

His love casts out all fear. He desires for us to be childlike; mature in Him, standing firm in faith, and filled with a peace that surpasses all understanding. My heart is learning to trust more in my God of hope. He will straighten every path and guide us home.

I have watched the movie *Pilgrim's Progress* and noticed similarities to my journey. There are times when it feels like we are at a standstill, with mountains blocking our way and hills to be moved. Then suddenly, it seems that we have progressed.

We often find ourselves in situations where we need to gather spiritual strength to sustain us until the end. Along the way, there may be people who try to hinder our progress as we journey towards the fulfilment of our earthly purpose.

May God grant us wisdom and discernment to know when to

rest and when to move forward, when to sit and when to stand, what to ask for, what to seek, and how to persevere, so that we may live according to God's perfect will. The Bible teaches us not to conform to the ways of this world, but be transformed by the renewing of our minds. That way, we may prove to ourselves the will of God which is good, acceptable and perfect.

We all need time and others to encourage us as we walk in this procession, but the Lord is with us and will never leave nor forsake us. He has promised us that. The Lord fills our mouths with His Word and through the Holy Spirit, He speaks through our mouths and speaks His truth to others.

Oh, I'm not underestimating this journey, my dear friends!

There have been times of weakness when I thought I wouldn't make it to the end. But greater is the Holy Spirit that is in me! My confidence is in the Lord, my God and King. If He says He will never leave us and is holding us, then our Lord and God will do so and fulfil His true promises. His Word cannot return void. That is why it's important to seek the answers we need concerning our lives from the Book of Truth – the Bible.

God is not a man that He should lie. He is in the spiritual realm - leading, guiding, and holding us. He ministers His truth, sometimes in a place of refuge where it can be just you and God as you build a personal relationship with Him.

Our God and King!

The Lord's help will continue to deepen our relationship with

In the Procession

our God of salvation. Without Him, this journey is worth nothing at all. We press on and forward for the reward to come.

May we stay focused and keep on track. Love is the most important thing of all as we journey through this life. May you receive His unconditional love today and be encouraged. May you never lose sight of the truth that you are loved, worthy and chosen. Even if your circumstances don't look like it, HOLD ON to the knowledge that Jesus Christ was sent on earth so that you may overcome and lead a life of abundance - earthly possessions and spiritual guidance.

As the pilgrimage continues, may the Lord lead you into the right places of rest and feeding, giving us strength and knowledge to do the will of our Holy Father. May He lead us to people He would like us to speak to, for His glory.

This life is only temporary, and we are only here for a while. May we make the best out of what we've been given and make sure to point others to our Lord Jesus Christ, so that they too will join in the procession with us. The way that leads to life is hard and very few will find it. May we enter by the narrow gate where Jesus Christ our Lord is the good shepherd.

For He does not abandon His sheep when they are in trouble. He has promised to deliver us from all our troubles.

Dear friends, do not give up your faith in Christ. May He give you ears that hear and listen to His clear instructions.

To Him be the glory forever and ever!

Lord, help us all to make it to the end. Keep us humble, keep us in your love. Help us, dear Lord, to make it to the end so that we may receive that great reward in heaven which is eternal life to come. In the name of Jesus hear our prayer.

Amen.

CHAPTER NINETEEN

When YES means YES and NO means NO!

There comes a time in our walk with Christ when we must realise that the time has come to say simply 'Yes' or 'No'. The Bible says,

> *"Just say 'Yes' or 'No'—anything else you say*
> *comes from the Evil One."*
>
> (Matthew 5:37)

The Lord Jesus Christ gave us words of His divine wisdom that came from above so that we don't keep sinning and be condemned on this journey. Where we are today on our pilgrims walk? Are we pressing in and being squeezed like a grape that is placed in the wine press?

God's Word has everything in it to help and guide us. Should we sit or stand or look into His perfect plan? Plans to prosper and give us peace and plans to help us walk with Him. It is all by faith that our human eyes cannot see, but God has a way of opening our spiritual eyes to see and ears to hear.

For faith comes by hearing the Word of God. It comes through hearing the teachings of the Bible which are true and cannot come back void when applied in our lives. We also learn the what, how, when and whys concerning the teachings we hear through truth-seeking preachers. It's impossible to have faith, let alone walk in faith if we don't HEAR THE WORD of God continuously.

Jesus told us to remain in His love and that His love will remain in us, remain in His Word and it will remain in us. Many times have I pondered on these words; at times going to His Word not knowing what to do, but searching for answers and revelations. Going to the Word of God is like digging for a treasure, until eventually the message enters into my heart, soul and spirit and makes me whole. There is transformation and renewal of the mind through the Holy Spirit as it teaches the truth of our Lord Jesus Christ.

Dear friends, I encourage you to never let go of God's goodness, no matter how dark things may seem in the world. He has given us His Word so that we can have an abundant life - walking and trusting in Him by faith and knowing that at the end of this life, there is a great reward to come, which is salvation and everlasting life.

Let us keep our eyes on the Author and Finisher of our faith in this life for eternal life. For Jesus Christ focused on the joy set before Him when He was crucified. He knew the reward to come - eternal life spent with His Father in Heaven. Let us look to Jesus today and consider His suffering far worse than ours. Still, God gave Him the strength to endure even unto death. Our Christ did endure suffering, pain, rejection, shame, and piercing and a crown of thorns was placed upon His head. He went through beating, whipping, spitting and mocking - all that we might have a life through our Lord Jesus.

Through Him, He is helping us to endure persecution, mocking and helping us through rejection, pain and suffering. He heals, including a mind that is troubled by things of the past such as abuse and beatings that caused us to gasp. And yet in it all, there is God's Word which is true and can heal us from suffering and help us to forgive.

Answers we don't always have when asked why God is allowing this suffering to happen. One thing I do know is that God is God and He can bring forth healing of the soul, body and spirit through Jesus Christ our Lord.

And leading a life of sin causes us much pain and suffering. I speak with encouragement after experiencing the cause and effect of sin. It would have destroyed me if God had not intervened, taken hold of my hand and showed me His forgiveness, love, mercy and compassion. Sometimes He disciplined and rebuked because He loves me so much.

Since then, God has taken me to places that I never knew; places where people are destitute, grieving and not knowing which way to turn. These are people from all nations, speaking different languages and belonging to different tribes, with skin colours different from mine.

This experience has opened me up to writing from my soul and heart every day, with the hope that someone will turn to God and never look back on their lives.

I have embraced writing from my soul and heart, hoping that someone will turn to God and never look back on their life. I did not have a pleasant childhood, but I found freedom in Christ later in life. Now, Christ has set me free, and I have become a servant of God, dedicated to doing His will on earth. I am no longer a slave to sin but a servant of God's righteousness!

All glory be to Him.

God has a way of transforming our pain into a passion —a passion to share with others so that through Jesus Christ, we can find a deep and fulfilling life. It requires a deep relationship in the depths of our being, and it demands everything we have.

Our 'Yes' must be genuine, and our 'No' must be definite, without boasting about our efforts. God knows the depths of our souls, hearts, and minds, and He searches them day and night until we find peace with Him through Jesus Christ. He brings us the peace of God.

He never lies or deceives to fulfil His will. He has warned us that there will be trials and troubles, but the good news is that the Lord has promised to deliver us from them all!

May we learn from the example of the Greatest King of all. He doesn't back down from His words of truth. He means what He says, and we can say 'Yes' and 'Amen' to all His promises! Never give up praying. Pray without ceasing and dedicate your lives to prayer. Paul the apostle encouraged all believers to be on guard. He wrote,

> *"Be alert, stand firm in the faith, be brave,*
> *be strong. Do all your work in love."*
>
> (1 Corinthians 16:13-14)

Not through words but by truth and action.

Do not be impressed with your wisdom or intelligence. These words are from Proverbs, reminding us that we are God's creation, meant to be used according to His will. Let's give glory to God, who is wise and powerful, as His work is within us and in the Church of Jesus Christ throughout all ages and the world without end.

Amen.

About the Author

Catherine Andrew's honest writing reflects her deep relationship with God. During a challenging period, she prayed for help and received guidance to "lay down and give in." Since then, she has learned to surrender, listen, and be guided by the Holy Spirit. She acknowledges the Holy Spirit as a gift from God to help her overcome severe mental anguish.

This is a collection of stories inspired by Catherine's experiences with God and her evolving relationship with the Lord as she grew in faith. Throughout her journey, Catherine has found healing, joy, and peace of mind. She is now dedicated to sharing her belief that God is real while highlighting the significance of Jesus Christ's sacrifice on the cross for all of us.

Catherine aims to help others discover and connect with God as a loving Father through His Begotten Son. At 69 years old, she is currently studying theology to strengthen her faith and inspire those who are lost or disheartened to return to Jesus Christ as a dependable shepherd.

*But God has shown us how much he loves us
—it was while we were still sinners that Christ died for us!*

(Romans 5:8)

Printed in Great Britain
by Amazon